Cambridge Elements

Elements in Translation and Interpreting
edited by
Kirsten Malmkjær
University of Leicester

CHARTING TRANSLATION RECEPTION

Methods and Challenges

Bei Hu
National University of Singapore

Shaftesbury Road, Cambridge CB2 8EA, United Kingdom

One Liberty Plaza, 20th Floor, New York, NY 10006, USA

477 Williamstown Road, Port Melbourne, VIC 3207, Australia

314–321, 3rd Floor, Plot 3, Splendor Forum, Jasola District Centre, New Delhi – 110025, India

103 Penang Road, #05–06/07, Visioncrest Commercial, Singapore 238467

Cambridge University Press is part of Cambridge University Press & Assessment, a department of the University of Cambridge.

We share the University's mission to contribute to society through the pursuit of education, learning and research at the highest international levels of excellence.

www.cambridge.org
Information on this title: www.cambridge.org/9781009569354
DOI: 10.1017/9781009569378

© Bei Hu 2025

This publication is in copyright. Subject to statutory exception and to the provisions of relevant collective licensing agreements, with the exception of the Creative Commons version the link for which is provided below, no reproduction of any part may take place without the written permission of Cambridge University Press & Assessment.

An online version of this work is published at doi.org/10.1017/9781009569378 under a Creative Commons Open Access license CC-BY-NC-ND 4.0 which permits re-use, distribution and reproduction in any medium for non-commercial purposes providing appropriate credit to the original work is given. You may not distribute derivative works without permission. To view a copy of this license, visit https://creativecommons.org/licenses/by-nc-nd/4.0

When citing this work, please include a reference to the DOI 10.1017/9781009569378

First published 2025

A catalogue record for this publication is available from the British Library

ISBN 978-1-009-56935-4 Hardback
ISBN 978-1-009-56939-2 Paperback
ISSN 2633-6480 (online)
ISSN 2633-6472 (print)

Cambridge University Press & Assessment has no responsibility for the persistence or accuracy of URLs for external or third-party internet websites referred to in this publication and does not guarantee that any content on such websites is, or will remain, accurate or appropriate.

For EU product safety concerns, contact us at Calle de José Abascal, 56, 1°, 28003 Madrid, Spain, or email eugpsr@cambridge.org

Charting Translation Reception

Methods and Challenges

Elements in Translation and Interpreting

DOI: 10.1017/9781009569378
First published online: October 2025

Bei Hu
National University of Singapore
Author for correspondence: Bei Hu, chsbei@nus.edu.sg

Abstract: This Element conceptualises translation reception as a form of cultural negotiation in which cognitive processes and sociocultural factors converge to form understanding. Drawing on empirical examples from a variety of translational phenomena, it maps a range of methodologies, including surveys, interviews, eye-tracking experiments, and big data analytics, to examine how heterogeneous reader expectations are either reconciled or divided. This Element argues that the ambiguities surrounding readers' identities and behaviours exemplify how reception thrives on paradoxes, uncertainties, and fluid boundaries. It proposes a nonlinear trade-off model to emphasise that mutual benefits in high-stakes communication can only be achieved when a requisite degree of trust is maintained among all stakeholders. This trust-based approach to translation reception provides us with the epistemological and methodological tools to navigate our post-truth multilingual world, where a new technocratic order looms. This title is also available as Open Access on Cambridge Core.

Keywords: translation reception, trust, user expectations, translation risk, cultural negotiation

© Bei Hu 2025

ISBNs: 9781009569354 (HB), 9781009569392 (PB), 9781009569378 (OC)
ISSNs: 2633-6480 (online), 2633-6472 (print)

Contents

Introduction: Thinking through Translation Reception   1

1 Why Does Translation Reception Matter?   5

2 User Expectations and Assessment   19

3 Approaches to Testing Reception in High-Stakes Communication   31

4 Conditioning Factors Underlying Translation Reception   44

5 Epilogue   55

References   57

Introduction: Thinking through Translation Reception

The act of a reader refining a text's potential into a specific meaning constitutes the process of reception. From a hermeneutic perspective, a text remains devoid of meaning until it is enlivened by the reader's interpretive response. The theory of reception in literary studies can be traced back to the Konstanz School, advanced by Wolfgang Iser and Hans-Robert Jauss and rooted in Gadamer's thinking with its later American offspring, shaping reader-response criticism and audience-focused hermeneutics. In this light, readers of all kinds actively construct meaning at the moment of reception, challenging traditional notions of an inherent or fixed ontological meaning in a (mediated) text (Martindale, 2006). Moving beyond the individual reader's response to a specific text, reception serves as an indicator of evolving norms in cultural relations and the broader processes of knowledge generation, prompting reflection on how meaning is (de)structured and how cultural boundaries can either be revealed or slowly melt away, often amid dispute.

However, in the parlance of translation studies, a traditional asymmetric focus was placed on producers over receivers. The field was long dominated by enquiries into the 'cause' underlying translation, with particular emphasis on the sociocultural and cognitive mechanisms that influenced a translator's choices. Most research on the production side virtually neglects how *actual readers* respond to translation strategies, which leads to a somewhat essentialist idea of what a good translation should be.

At its best, without empirical evidence on reception, translation becomes a process in which the translator conjures an (often idealised) 'implied reader' who subtly influences every decision made. Although the translator's own horizon is often seen as partial or restricted in contrast to that of the actual reader, many foundational theories in translation insist that a text carries within it the echoes of imaginary effects inscribed upon individuals and society alike. Given such mawkish idealisations of readerships, actual readers fail to generate adequate attention, as comparatively limited attention has been given to examining the often-great gulf between what is empirically received by readers and what was initially expected on the production side. This takes the investigation of translation effects from a descriptive account to a somewhat prescriptive stance.

Resistance to considering reception in translation studies is gradually fading and falling away, but its full embrace still eludes the field. The triumph of deconstructive postmodernism heralded the end of a definitive understanding of the text itself; more recently, there has been a discernible shift in scholarly interest in the 'effects' of translation. The flipside of 'dethroning' the source text is the idea of prioritising how translated texts are interpreted, rewritten, reimagined, and represented within their target contexts. Such a move away from an ontological preoccupation with the translator and towards an exploration of the target-side dynamics signifies a critical evolution in the epistemological and empirical frameworks of translation studies. Meaning is actualised and made real at the moment of being received. In this sense, reception reifies translation.

Nevertheless, sui generis models devoted to reception have remained underdeveloped (Tuominen, 2018). All too often, they remain relegated to the margins, are not subjected to systematic investigation, and often lack a robust theoretical scaffolding that has been directly corroborated by empirical evidence (Kruger & Kruger, 2017). The study of translation effects, as Chesterman (1998) argued, remains encumbered by untested assumptions regarding readers and the impact of specific translation solutions on the target side. One plausible explanation is that the ambiguous reader remains a nontrivial challenge. Unlike the relatively smaller and more controlled community of translators, who are often certified or vetted based on specific criteria, the readership on the reception side is far more complex, elusive, and, in many ways, evanescent.

While many translation scholars (though not necessarily the majority) have happily embraced a broader vision that transcends the printed word and extends to audio-visual media, dynamic texts, and interpreting, the reader remains the true enigma. Readers are 'notoriously elusive', remarks Athique (2016: 6), whose presence is both ephemeral and profoundly influential. Their linguistic and cultural belongings converge into what Jauss (1982) evocatively described as a 'horizon of expectations', a fluid, ever-shifting cognitive template that frames the construction of meaning. In this context, 'reader' is used as an inclusive concept, encompassing all those who receive translated works in various modalities, whether as readers of written texts, listeners in interpretive events, users of machine translations, or audiences of dynamic audio-visual content. Rather than accentuating the distinctions between these groups, the focus is on highlighting the shared grounds that underpin the ways in which individuals engage with the process of translation. Their expectations, at once distinct and at times paradoxically contradictory, defy any universal approach. Needless to say, readers are not a homogeneous set. This has consistently bedevilled attempts to reach a consensus on reception, making a one-size-fits-all translation nothing but illusory quicksand, given the idiosyncratic, situated, and contingent character of readings.

Nonetheless, testing translation effects and reader responses is essential because it evaluates the efficacy of translational communication without relying on the impractical notion of ideal readerships with homogeneous and unbiased expectations. In Chesterman's (1998) twofold taxonomy of translation's impact on individual readers, primary effects manifest as shifts in mental state, including both emotional and cognitive responses, while secondary effects emerge as behavioural changes influencing actions, knowledge, comprehension, and aesthetic experience. Building on this foundation, H. Kruger (2016) introduced the notion of tertiary effects, perceiving translation as a force with sociocultural and ideological reverberations. In this view, the fundamental 'lower' cognitive processes serve as the necessary underpinnings for the 'higher' cultural dynamics that translation entails (Kruger & Kruger, 2017: 72).

The varied levels of defining translation reception may explain why different methodological epistemologies have been applied to different categories of readership, usually using temporal proximity as a scale. When a text takes a long time to reach its intended audience, it is hardly surprising that reception studies are more likely to explore its broader, long-term societal impact. For instance, literary texts are translated for imagined readers whose expectations seem rather elusive and whose profiles are blurred. Literary translators scratch out words, translate the text, and, rolling the dice, submit it to the editor before the publisher's long-awaited move into the market. In the tenet of literary reception, the research focus has been largely rooted in broader social traditions and cultural genealogies, focusing on how the translation is affected by prevalent expectancy norms that designate whether target readers would be enamoured with them.

In contrast, when a text in an interpreting event reaches its audience in the immediacy of the moment, the research focus of its reception often lies in analysing the audience's immediate cognitive reactions, making empirical and experimental investigations stand as the cornerstones of methodology. Interpreters are reliant on their listeners, if not for direct praise, then at least for the absence of criticism, as negative feedback poses risks to their professional standing (Cheung, 2020).

In more complicated scenes with multiple readerships across spatial and temporal axes, one particularly intriguing example is the translation of texts on foreign affairs in China. Chinese institutional translators do not specifically address target-culture readers outside of China; instead, they see their supervisors as their first and most powerful readers (Hu, 2020). The psychological effect in this case is to erase the image of an external receiver, prompting Chinese translators' tendency to write in the house style and to adopt the established terms and jargon of the foreign discourse system, however opaque or inaccessible such language may be to general readers.

Of course, all these summaries, with a touch of relativism, might be considered oversimplifications of complicated intercultural receptions. As such, our analytic models should not be restricted to scrutinising translation reception at one or two levels and must, instead, be conceptualised as a comprehensive, systemic process of socio-cognitive engineering.

Moreover, the need persists to address the reductionist view of trivialising reception as a quality assessment, which raises fundamental questions about how reception works. This is not to decry the examination of translation quality and certainly not to excoriate the save-the-world aim of pursuing excellence. The stakes of the game are that, in contrast to assessment, which is endowed with a sense of definitive authority, reception is relative, circumstantial, and less deterministic, focusing on open-ended, actual complexity rather than on an idealised certainty envisaged in the professional's mind. For instance, for some critics, investigations into user expectations largely prioritise the evaluations of professional users, such as peer interpreters, above those of end users (Liu, 2023). Despite these self-evident advancements, the perspectives, experiences, and reception of the *end users* in varying setups remain virtually underexplored, emphasising a critical void in existing scholarship.

Reception has value by bringing to the conscious mind the factors that may realise the text's full potential and exerting societal influence when the translation is cognitively processed by readers and elicits substantive effects. A translation and its reception are always implicated in one another and in dialogue. Reception can be fragmented and, at times, polyphonic. Pressing issues must be faced in an interdisciplinary way, not only confined to academia but also viewed amid the collaboration linking practitioners, translators, and diverse multilingual communities. In our post-truth era, when distrust casts a long shadow over communication, it becomes imperative to critically examine the risks that high-stakes messaging poses to our collective dialogue, particularly in the digital age.

A good part of this Element challenges some of the more reductive interpretations of translation reception, beginning with an exploration of why the study of reception is essential. Following this, we provide a critical overview of current developments to contextualise recent research on user expectations and evaluative practices within translation studies. Our initial focus is on heterogeneous readerships, examining expectancy norms, socio-cognitive frameworks, and considerations of usability and accessibility. Subsequently, we turn to a synoptic view of reception methodologies that assess reader comprehension, as well as the acceptability and actionability of multimodal texts. This section emphasises the methodological strengths and limitations of various approaches, supplemented by illustrative examples and comparative analyses. We then investigate the factors that condition translation reception, including language, cultural relations, trust, technological mediation, and power dynamics among hierarchical readerships. The Element concludes with future research directions, with particular attention to fostering trust in the convergence of languages, cultures, and technologies, which is considered essential in addressing the epistemological complexities of a post-truth multilingual world.

1 Why Does Translation Reception Matter?

1.1 Making Connections

The idea of reception arises partly from the impetus imparted to the discipline of classics from European and American literary theories of the 1960s, which bestowed a key role on readers, emphasising the aesthetic significance of literary works. The *locus classicus* of reception theory includes Hans-Robert Jauss's 'horizon of expectations', delineating the cultural norms that influence readers' understanding and judgement of classically oriented literary works. Wolfgang Iser's emphasis on the reader is a vital presence in filling gaps and deriving meaning from text. In a similar vein, the reader-response criticism championed by American theorist Stanley Fish challenges historical determinism by affirming the aesthetic responses of contemporary readers.

For translation scholars, this shift towards reader-centric perspectives, underlining the interpretive aspect of communicating, diverges from the prior emphasis on linguistic equivalence as the primary measure of translation quality, and instead advocates for understanding translations as socio-linguistically constrained texts influenced by their reception in the target context. Here, we use the term 'text' in its extended poststructuralist sense – a concept that accommodates not only traditional written works but also films, interpreted press conferences, and even government health messages.

Long-held assumptions regarding the inherent superiority of original texts have been questioned, paving the way for the recognition of new interpretations as possessing their own independent value. For instance, Nida's groundbreaking idea of dynamic equivalence (Nida & Taber, 2003 [1969]) asserts that the original message must be rendered in the receptor language to evoke an effect akin to that experienced by the original audience. Similarly, target-oriented functionalist theories posit that the needs and expectations of end users are paramount in selecting appropriate strategies and assessing a translation's success (Nord, 2005; Reiss & Vermeer, 1984). In this light, the focus slowly but firmly shifts to the reader, whose mental senses are integral to the translator's decision-making process. The act of reception invites a new perspective on the purpose of translation, anchoring its potential within the infinite plurality of reader expectations.

However, classical translation theories have often treated readers in passing, regarding the target side as a mere formality without fully engaging its agency and complexity. While reception theory has concentrated on literary works and the act of reading (cf. Michelakis, 2006), the dynamics of actual readers in understanding texts across diverse modalities remains largely unexplored. For instance, when Newmark (1988: 133–134) proposed that 'the translator must take into account all aspects involving readership sensitivity in order to stimulate the appropriate frame of mind in the reader', the British translation scholar remarked that what should be translated are the words themselves, since 'all that is there, on the page', rejecting the idea of texts being interpretive constructions. Consider the somewhat problematic argument: It creates the illusion that one could peer through a viewfinder at a text, as if the sole version that truly matters is the fixed, uncontaminated original, leaving various forms of essentialism within translation unquestioned for the most part.

In reality, the final image (the 'translation') is constructed by more than the viewfinder (the 'translator') through which the act of looking ('translating') occurs. Numerous theories of translation exist, in terms of both competence and in ethical practice, that grapple with the enduring, essentialist legacy of what constitutes 'a good translation'. The trouble with such formulations is that many of them are not empirically tested on the actual reader. Fewer have attempted to theorise how reception has the potential to address the long-standing prescriptivism within translation studies, a discipline that traditionally prescribes what constitutes an 'ethical' translation and offers normative judgments on translators.

For instance, consider Borges's notion of 'frivolous superstition', expressed through his vehement repudiation of any deviation from Don Quixote introduced during the act of translation (Lianeri, 2006). Phillip E. Lewis's notion of 'abusive fidelity' (1985/2012) celebrates translations that eschew target-culture norms and adhere so rigidly to the original that the text retains an exotic, almost foreign flavour. Such translations serve as a kind of teaching tool – a humble crib – that aids readers in unravelling the original meaning without assimilation. This concept mirrors Venuti's idea of resistance translation; however, to date, little empirical work has been done to assess these assumptions in real readers. This is no new insight. As Kruger and Kruger (2017) pointed out, when cognitive theoretical frameworks, such as Fillmore's (1977) scenes-and-frames and Muñoz's (2010) embodied cognition, find applications in translation reception, they are rarely evaluated against empirical evidence.

My contention is that the central dictum of reception research is a more critical understanding of the reading experience, when the interaction between text and reader emerges. That said, the contingent and fluid meaning of translation, though shrouded in concealment, is eventually unearthed and reconfigured, emerging in a voice that speaks in the reader's own terms. Here, my intention is to draw attention to theoretical frameworks emerging from diverse research traditions, ranging from written translation, interpreting, to audio-visual media. The aim is to show how the study of readers' engagement with texts holds greater commonality than is typically recognised, offering potential for mutual enrichment and intellectual cross-fertilisation. For instance, approaching the audio-visual translation (AVT) and drawing on Janet Staiger's (2005) conceptualisation, Elena Di Giovanni (2018) emphasised the need to clearly define the primary object of investigation. She differentiated perception from reception, noting that, in media studies, perception often refers to visual impressions formed when viewing media content. In broad strokes, perception reaches its conclusion before any acts of interpretation or appreciation begin, acts that belong instead to the realm of reception. Despite the challenges posed by text genres, diverse audience demographics, language pairs, directionality, and broader sociocultural and ideological constraints, what remains to be seen is precisely how reception accounts for the manner in which a text is 'interpreted, valued, and remembered' (Di Giovanni, 2018: 161).

1.2 Moving to the Target Side

Since the 1980s, when translation studies carved out their own identity, scholars have shifted from a predominantly linguistic approach centred on notions of equivalence and textual comparison to an enquiry that situates translation within the cultural reservoir of its effect. This marked a watershed moment in the study of translation reception, opening avenues to explore how translation influences identity formation and reflects the sociocultural dynamics of the target culture. More broadly, research on language and linguistic continuity has transcended mere textual concerns towards the process of socially constructed and collectively endorsed ideas, thereby ratifying Angelelli's (2014) 'sociological turn' in the field.

Unlike their literary counterparts, translation scholars have been more at ease moving beyond the timeless bonds between an antecedent text and its historical receptions, embracing a presentist perspective that acknowledges the experiences and immediate realities of contemporary readers. A wealth of theoretical frameworks and constructs are rooted in target-oriented paradigms, relating texts to modern readers' concerns – such as the Skopos theory, audience design, translation norms, and risk management – albeit occasionally lacking explicit acknowledgement of the reception nomenclature.

Influenced by Toury's (1995/2012, see also Toury 1980) target-oriented descriptive approach to translation, reception is typically framed in expansive cultural rhetoric, such as the question of 'how a translation functions in the recipient culture'. Much of the translation research in this vein, emerging in the twilight of the twentieth century, was devoted to illustrating the role of translation within broader cultural systems. Scholars have examined how prevailing norms sculpt translational choices and, in turn, how these choices play out within the receiving culture (Chesterman, 1993, 1998). For norm descriptivists, the receiver's expectations play a decisive role in shaping translational choices and defining what constitutes a 'good' translation from conceptual, evaluative, and affective perspectives (see Chesterman, 1993; Halverson & Kotze, 2022; Kotze et al., 2021).

Notably, this target-oriented focus is intrinsically linked to the supraindividual reception of translated texts. Scholars have long probed the position of translated literature within the broader literary system (Chang 2011; Even-Zohar, 1978), suggesting that it may assume either a central or a peripheral role within a target culture. This dynamic resonates with Jauss's notion of 'aesthetic distance'. Drawing on Even-Zohar's framework of cultural repertoire, Andringa (2006) reimagined repertoire as 'mental equipment', a set of values and principles that guides evaluation and judgement. In essence, the study of translation transcends its mere textual production to include the various judgements cast upon its quality, its educational or religious implications, and its overall reception. For example, research on reception has leveraged the concept of paratext – a term coined by Genette (1997) to denote both the internal elements of a book and those external features that surround it – to illustrate how texts are received. These paratextual cues appear in book reviews, articles, columns, blogs, and in public discourses and personal communications, each throwing slivers of light on the reception process. A handful of studies grounded in empirical data (Baer, 2014; Batchelor, 2018; Chen, 2022a, 2024; Escudero, 2022; Neveu, 2017) have scrutinised the key role that paratext plays in shaping the reception of translated works.

Beyond text, the turn of the millennium saw a gradual shift in norm research towards agents central to the reception side, such as publishers, translators, critics, and academics. These agents are the axis of the consolidation or dismantling of translation norms, shaping shared socio-cognitive frameworks that inform how translations are conceptualised and construed retrospectively (see Hu, 2020; Meylaerts, 2008; Milton & Bandia, 2009; Sela-Sheffy, 2005). Translations are refashioned during the process of norm making and breaking. They are continually reconfigured in the crucible of reception, and their meanings are refashioned by interpretation. In this way, a key virtue of reception lies in a deconstructionist commitment to pluralism.

Influenced by deconstruction and grounded in the premise that the reader actively constructs the meaning of a (literary) text, Baer (2014) explored the unique 'readerliness' of translated works. By questioning the perceived supremacy of the source text and its author, this postpositivist approach to reading emancipates translation from rigid, language-based paradigms that relegate it to a mere shadow of the original. Instead of relying on the Platonic ideals of equivalence and fidelity, Baer champions diverse voices, contexts, and readerships that translation brings forth, advocating that translation can enrich and complicate the reading experience in dynamic and generative ways.

Let this underline a further point of perplexity: One may argue that the target-side paradigm conjures the spectre of moral scepticism ('Why should we care about laypersons' understanding of a text? It's just a matter of personal opinion') or cultural relativism. Here, as elsewhere, the question of a tripartite model of reception can prompt some interesting answers. Although empirical studies on translation reception have examined Chesterman's (1998) primary and secondary effects – specifically, individuals' cognitive and emotional states and behaviours – there has been limited exploration of real readers' responses to translations through the lens of Chesterman's tertiary effects. As Pym (2020: 453) poignantly observes, '[w]e know remarkably little about how readers construe translations'. One may suggest that the tertiary effects in question incorporate the prevailing expectation norms and cognitive-evaluative frameworks of specific cultural milieus while simultaneously revealing *how* readers' responses transform these paradigms. The spontaneous, bottom-up workings of the mind converge with top-down social influences, melding unconscious cognitive impulses with cultural forces that ultimately govern translation reception.

Reception studies tend to coalesce around specific domains, favouring topics like literary translation, interpreting, and dynamic texts, while addressing themes of cultural relativism, translation strategies, and risk management. Predominant variables, such as cognitive effort and reading patterns, further constitute the discourse, forming a constellation of ideas to which we shall return later.

1.3 Reception from a Sociocultural Perspective

Any attempt to grasp translation reception must grapple with two intertwined questions: First, how should we examine it; and second, why choose one method over another? While no single, universal paradigm can capture all the nuances of translation reception, several overarching parameters have emerged, chief among them a classic framework with a decidedly sociological focus.

Examining translation reception from a social perspective compels us to articulate rationales for its inherent societal embeddedness. Viewed thus, reception is a socially constructed phenomenon, conditioned by interpretations and conventions anchored in specific contexts. It invites renewal through the very act of communication and fostering cultural self-definition. This approach is especially pertinent in the case of retranslations (Işıklar Koçak & Erkul Yağcı, 2019; Wang & Humblé, 2020; Wardle, 2019), where evolving aesthetic judgements and shifting cultural values further compound the process.

The reception of written literary translations is often conceptualised through frameworks derived from some 'postclassical' variants of structuralist narratology, an approach that seeks to unearth an underlying narrative architecture founded upon universal syntax (Rimmon-Kenan, 2002; Kruger, 2009). For instance, Chatman's (1978) seminal model of narrative communication identifies four textual participants: the implied author, the implied reader, the narrator, and the narratee. Here, the narrator is the voice that tells the story, while the narratee is the figure to whom the story is addressed. More crucially, the implied author embodies the values and voice inherent in the text, and the implied reader represents the audience that the text presupposes. This approach has long influenced reception research in translation (Bosseaux, 2007), drawing attention to how the concept of the implied reader can influence a translator's decision-making. However, in literary reception, the actual reader is often rendered invisible, reduced to an abstract role that stands apart from the tangible realities of the real author and genuine readership, and consequently marginalised in literary analysis.

The polysystemic approach to literary and poetical translations prompts us to consider how and why translated texts are positioned within central or peripheral roles in the target culture. Equally intriguing is the view of translations as instruments of fairness, accessibility, and justice for language minorities, prompting us to examine their place in the broader currents of cultural formation, at times from an activist standpoint. For instance, Baker (2006), the firebrand standard-bearer of translation activism, challenges us with her evocative call to examine 'frame' and 'framing', looking into how personal and collective narratives reconfigure discourse in translational activities. For Baker, the power of narratives is not solely framed at creation but is continuously reconstituted through reception, with the reader emerging as the pivotal fulcrum for narrative discourse analysis.

In a similar vein, imagology is gaining a prominent role in reception practice and analysis, especially when social traditions intersect or are in conflict. Imagology, primarily developed within comparative literature, examines the discursive representation of national, cultural, or ethnic identities, focusing on how nations and nationalities are portrayed and reinforced rather than their essence. While traditionally applied to literary texts, imagology has also proven insightful for translations of journalistic writing, children's literature, and travel writing, in which mediated narratives are constantly received as an enactment of identity. Despite globalisation, attributing national and cultural characteristics, if not stereotypes, remains a prevalent method of categorising reading behaviour and perceptions, with binary categories like North–South and East–West often reinforcing the gloom of prejudices, stereotypes, and ethnocentrism (van Doorslaer, 2024).

Despite the predominance in current research of reader expectations and responses in social contexts, a notable gap remains: The precise nexus between the sociocultural (macro-level) dimension of translation reception and the individual reader's cognitive and linguistic (micro-level) engagement remains elusive. Although Baer (2014) has called for solitary readers to coalesce into interpretive communities, such efforts in translation studies are tenuous. As Kruger and Kruger (2017) observe, the contested terrain where individual and communal facets of reception converge has seen few attempts to theorise their interconnectedness. This oversight does little justice to the complexities of translational dynamics and neglects the fact that reception is an evolving phenomenon, one that eludes the confines of linear, diachronic time.

One notable exception to this general reticence to theorizing the convergence of reception is offered by Kruger (2016). Appealing to contextualist, cognitive, psychonarratological, and reader-response approaches, in her analysis of children's literature translation, Kruger examines how readers construct textual features and explores how manipulated textual devices in translations influence reception by affecting comprehension, narrative construction, attitudes, and emotions, as well as reading experiences. Recent contributions by Kotze (Kotze et al., 2021; see also Halverson & Kotze, 2022) further introduce the cognitive-evaluative template as a favoured trope in reception research. Tymoczko (2012) similarly advocates for the neuroscience of translation, emphasising the crucial links between the fine-grained workings of individual cognition and the far-reaching forces exerted by language, culture, and ideological slants.

Methodologically, these approaches have extended the study of reader response into empirical and experimental enquiry across diverse translation modes. This shift is especially resonant as AVT flourishes alongside evolving cognitive narratology. Notably, the notion of psychological immersion has proven to be a powerful tool, illuminating how subtitles can usher audiences into the very essence of the filmic story world.

Another most fruitful area for studying the culmination of efforts to integrate cognitive and sociocultural approaches lies in 'digital social reading' (Rebora et al., 2021: 230; Rowberry, 2016), which hubristically echoes the 'sociological turn' in translation reception to empower readers. Recent studies have investigated the nature of reader interaction and the impact of collaborative dialogue on individual reception, particularly in digital spaces. For instance, Jiménez-Crespo (2011) explored how translation quality assessments galvanised a vibrant community of Facebook users. He found that individuals not only cast votes on proposed translations but also crystallised enduring online dialogues, contributing to a collective evaluation by professional translators. In Chen's (2022) application of a cognitive-social approach to online readers' engagement with translations, the author explores readers' cognitive understanding, attitudes, and expectations, framing translation reception as an affective experience and a subject of evaluation and critique in online forums. In the end, the translator–reader online exchange is transformed into an evolving form of social communion that reflects our deeper yearning to connect, interpret, and be understood.

In the digital era, reception is no longer confined to individual interpretation; it has developed into a communal ritual wherein texts become the catalysts for ongoing dialogue (Allington, 2007). From this point, one can presume an egalitarian politics of reception, which nurtures a collective engagement that enriches the shared cultural experience. This process, admittedly, is never without its tensions, as disputes and conflicting views are ever in flux, awaiting reconciliation in dialogue. Such dynamics arise from the diverse expectations of readers and the hierarchical power structures that affect their interactions, a point to be discussed in the following section.

1.4 Reception from a Cognitive Dimension

Promising theorisations on reception emerge from the confluence of cognitive–linguistic enquiry and macro-cognitive narratology, enriched further by insights from psychological immersion, reading research, and usability and accessibility studies. Central to this exploration is the pioneering concept of cognitive frames. Rooted in Fillmore's seminal scenes-and-frames semantics, this notion was later introduced into translation studies by Snell-Hornby (2005). A cognitive frame operates as a constellation of rhetorical decisions that both ignite and bind the mental scene, conjuring a vividly experienced scenario within the reader's mind (Kruger & Kruger, 2017). According to Snell-Hornby (2005: 195), the frame can be seen as a dynamic process driven by allusive and alluding meanings, where the roles of the author, the translator (who simultaneously reads the original and crafts the target text) and the eventual reader engage in a constant, reciprocal exchange. When these scenes and frames continuously ignite one another in the audience's consciousness, they can evoke a sudden frisson of sense making that transcends ordinary understanding. Extending this perspective, Muñoz (2010) emphasised the role of embodied cognition, suggesting that the interpretation of a text is intimately connected with the translator's embodied experiences. In theory, in their quest to render meaning, translators deftly balance the diverse expectations and needs of the target reader.

Contemporary approaches to the cognitive analysis of reception, whether at the microsystemic or macrosystemic level, have increasingly converged. The convergence between the individual and the collective, echoing the Fishian model of reception, has prompted reader expectations to be systematically excavated and brought to consciousness. Linking these concerns and underpinning them is a form of *social* cognition that enables translators to discern the author's intentions while situating the audience's requirements. This evaluative process forms the bedrock of translational strategies, bridging the sectarian divide between cognitive analysis and social norms.

There is renewed curiosity about how the psychological and emotional states of readers are associated with the sociocultural framing of translation. Although we lack an Archimedean point from which to definitively settle how readers forge connections with texts across time, empirical studies have begun to explore how translation can, in effect, establish a collective cultural memory. Cross (2018) opined that our recollections of childhood and adolescence may be more psychological than historical, which is imbued with a timeless quality. In her exploration of reader nostalgia, Chen (2023) found that a translation encountered in youth often transforms into an idealised relic, its timeless charm intensifying its favourability in later years. Chen (2023) contended that an earlier version of a translation may crystallise into a collective memory of one's formative years, leading adult readers to resist subsequent iterations, albeit implicitly. When nostalgia enters the fray, the evaluation of a translation is inevitably imbued with subjective emotion.

Nostalgia offers a provocative new lens through which to view the aging process in retranslation research. The wistful longing for earlier translations complicates deterministic notions of a linear, terminal progression, instead priming the reception of new texts against the backdrop of collective memory. In this view, the original translation serves as a vital frame of reference – a mental model – against which subsequent versions are measured (Chen, 2023). Such findings challenge the prevalent hypothesis that translations inevitably decay over time, necessitating retranslation (Berman, 1990: 1–2), and serve as a telling testament to how cognitive reception actively articulates a text's sociocultural resonance.

In parallel, recent reception research has placed as much weight on the cognitive processes of *individual* readers to understand how various aspects of a translation explicitly impact readers' actual responses (or 'perceptual decoding'), comprehension, and evaluations (Díaz Cintas & Szarkowska, 2020). In the empirical cognitive reception paradigm, the focus centres on how individuals internalise texts through cognitive processes, with affective responses acknowledged as part of the overall engagement (Kruger & Kruger, 2017). Departing from the notion of a homogeneous readership, on an empirical quest for the 'real' reader's cognitive load, enjoyment, and immersion, this cognitive approach is graphically evident in the context of the sheer breadth and diversity of audio-visual texts as an object of research (Di Giovanni & Gambier, 2018).

For instance, Aleksandrowicz (2020) examines how cognitive and individual responses influence the reception of film music in subtitles for deaf and hard-of-hearing audiences. By presenting film clips with different subtitling strategies, ranging from mood descriptions to detailed composer information, this reception study examines how viewers process emotional cues in the absence of sound. The findings indicate that despite variations in subtitle content, viewers' emotional reactions remain largely consistent, suggesting that the cognitive processes underlying emotion recognition rely on integrated visual and textual information. Thus, individual cognitive engagement emerges as a vital mediator in the reception of audio-visual content, offering empirical support for embodied cognition in the richness and complexity of meaning making in subtitled media.

In addition, defined as the profound sensation of presence, a state of being entirely absorbed in a fictional reality (Kruger & Doherty, 2018), the concept of immersion rooted in virtual reality studies has served as another exemplified model of bridging cognitive and social chasms in translation reception. Scholars suggest that the convergence of visual and auditory stimuli, coupled with the resonant cadences of prosody, can elevate immersion by evoking powerful emotional responses and language processing (Cohen et al., 2006). Szarkowska and Boczkowska (2022) set out to examine how colour coding influences viewers' reception, focusing on immersion, comprehension, and cognitive load. The findings revealed that colour coding appears to benefit viewers who are typically less prone to immersion in a film's narrative. A more recent study (Szarkowska et al., 2024) examined how incongruities between dialogue and subtitles impact cognitive load, enjoyment, and overall viewing experience. The results showed that incongruities led to a slightly higher cognitive load and reduced enjoyment, but they did not compromise comprehension. Moreover, viewers engage with audio-visual content not merely for passive entertainment but to experience a transcendent pleasure, which is an affective process sparked by intimate affiliations with characters and the unfolding destinies they embody (Tamborini, 2010).

Nevertheless, most reception research on immersion and enjoyment has been confined to monolingual settings, leaving us with a scant understanding of how comprehension and cognitive load are embedded in the process of intralingual translation reception. Admittedly, the attempts to formulate generalisable hypotheses about cognitive reception mirror earlier scholarly attention to social reception. Both approaches, in their ambition, have too often swept many complexities under the rug, leaving nuances unexplored.

Considering advances in digital technology, such as the growing use of eye-tracking techniques and computational big data analytics, empirically focused reception research is steadily making inroads into translation studies. Technology-driven methodologies and visual representations undeniably resonate with modern appetites. Moreover, the concept of 'experimental studies of translation reception' (Walker, 2021: 482) is gathering momentum. This embryonic paradigm contends that by subjecting translation reception to experimental investigation, we can uncover how specific translation strategies modulate the cognitive load on readers and impact broader social and cultural life. In doing so, it seeks to understand the diverse outcomes produced by various translation approaches and the differential effects observed between source and target texts at both individual and societal levels. This convergent trend invites us to re-examine translation reception, a confluence where cognitive processes and cultural forces merge, continually shaping meaning in a perpetual evolution.

1.5 Why Test Translation Reception?

A question worth asking is whether the notion of 'reception' as a catch-all term still holds currency in our era, especially when its definition ignites debate over its scope and methodology. Simon Goldhill (2002: 297), a classics scholar, once remarked that the term is 'too blunt, too passive' to encapsulate the vibrant dance of resistance, assimilation, and self-aggrandisement observed in cultural processes. While his critique may have its merits, we must recall that 'reception' was chosen (consciously and deliberately) in lieu of alternatives such as 'the (classic) original' or 'fidelity' to suggest the dynamic, imaginative role played by the receiver.

The vexing question is best approached by stepping back to appreciate the enduring potency of translation as hermeneutic. Meanings and interpretations often intersect. No translated text legitimates an essentialist truth that can be faithfully or equivalently conveyed. Instead, all texts remain open to being understood, perpetually necessitating engagement between *people*, and meaning is continually reconstructed with each act of reception, constituting a dynamic process of sense making. Reception studies unsettle the complacent certainty that truth exists as a fixed binary, either here or there, and invite us instead to consider true values as fluid characterised by context and interpretation. Along these anti-essentialist lines, translation reception entails the mediated interaction between authors, translators, readers and all kinds of agents involved. Various theoretical tenets in translation studies invoke concepts intrinsic to the target side, implying that a translation's true effectiveness is eventually measured by the critical engagement of reader responses, reactions, and lasting reverberations (Gambier, 2018).

Pragmatic matters offer additional reasons to study reception, given the overwhelmingly 'accessible' character of contemporary translations. With Kovačič's (1995) pioneering call for more attention to reader reception that emphasised the assessment of translated texts, followed by Suojanen, Koskinen, and Tuominen's (2015) user-centred approach to translation, a new awareness emerged, positing that evaluation-based reception research can refine translation strategies and tactics through empirical testing. As with Kovačič, such reception-based critiques can critically assess the effectiveness of audience design and challenge unverified assumptions about the needs and expectations of 'real readers'. Reception research, therefore, has the potential to provide translators with guidance by giving an assessment of the right action, countering reliance on assumptions often rooted in individual biases and stereotypes, thereby developing a more informed and systematic approach to translation.

Reception is pedagogical and much more besides. By studying reception, we question those cold-headed, irrefutable arguments and prescriptive theories rooted in the production side of translation, which is a challenging, but rewarding, line of enquiry to pursue further. For example, in retranslation studies, the axiom that 'new equals improved' is widely held (Deane-Cox, 2014: 48). This reflects a linear vision of the development of translation history as always a continual progression in which reinterpretation is essential to breathe fresh life into the original text, ensuring that it remains vibrant and relevant. According to such progressivist narratives, only retranslations can produce a 'great translation' by fully revealing and reproducing the original meaning (Berman, 1990: 7). However, comparing reader responses and reviews of different versions of E.B. White's *Charlotte's Web* (1952), Chen (2023) noted that childhood nostalgia influences the reception of retranslations. Despite the lower quality of Xin Kang's earlier translation in the late 1970s, many readers still prefer it to Rongrong Ren's widely available retranslation around the turn of the millennium. This preference stems from readers' collective memories associated with Kang's version, suggesting that knowledge can be received as a form of attachment. This empirical study echoes Koskinen and Paloposki's (2015) observation that ardent aficionados and ordinary readers often favour the inaugural translation, even when subsequent versions virtually receive acclaim from publishers and professional critics.

While the actual reader of the translated text has been brought into focus within the research agenda, the primary and secondary effects of reception (Chesterman, 1998), such as the cognitive and behavioural effects of translations on readers, are given priority. More recent scholarship has further developed Chesterman's ideas, suggesting that a holistic integration with the tertiary effects of translation (in other words, the sociocultural and ideological connotations of translation) is indispensable. Some emphasis has been placed on the way in which cognitive responses might steadily contribute to cultural formations, with H. Kruger (2012: 266) pointing out that cognitive load might not be necessarily be negative per se, as it may offer pedagogical virtues that eventually lead to 'gains in the development of greater lexical, pragmatic, and cultural knowledge'.

Charting translation reception involves (re)examining the give-and-take between translators and their readers, particularly on the cusp of world-changing technologies when innumerable new readings and new readerships are generated, altering the texture of reading practices. The complex chain of reception of new forms of dynamic texts, such as streaming media content, viewing and dubbing in a digital landscape, has gained traction (Pavesi, 2019). In an analysis of *danmu*-assisted back translation,[1] which is an on-screen subtitling method applied to a classical English-subtitled Chinese drama on a streaming platform, Chen (2023) noticed that such back translations have been repurposed as a tool for Chinese viewers to acquire English through a dynamic media counterflow. When combined with the original dubbed or subtitled texts and the video's visual elements, *danmu* subtitles create a participatory 'third space' (Bhabha, 1994) that offers language learners an engaging, interactive environment. Likewise, Pym and Hu (2022) explored how Australian-based Chinese-speaking users engaged in impassioned debates on social media about COVID-19 translations, arguing that trust in vaccination was forged not solely by the presentation of official translations in our post-democratic age, but through the dialogic process of reception.

On the other hand, although the target-oriented emphasis on the reader has gained increasing recognition, the systematic examination and assessment of

---

[1] The term *danmu* (or *danmaku*, meaning 'barrage' or 'bullet curtain' in Japanese) refers to the interface and overlaid, time-synced comments that streak across video images as users watch such content (Li, 2017).

recipients' responses remains largely unexplored. Our goal is not merely to capture a transient glimpse of the *text*'s eternal verities – crudely speaking – but to analyse and synthesise the collective views and underlying intentions of the *people*.

Indeed, reception research seems to compel the conclusion that our understanding of cross-cultural content is invariably constrained and contextualised by our beliefs about, or even our ignorance of, the reader. The evolution of media, technology, and ideological conflicts has only served to deepen the complexity of reader profiles. As Pöchhacker (2018) notes, user-based studies have crystallised around two principal themes: the quality expectations and assessments of users, and audience preferences and comprehension regarding (media) accessibility. Reception research now recognises that readers are a heterogeneous mosaic underpinned by diverse linguistic and demographic backgrounds, shifting cultural relations, and new media modalities. For instance, Li (2024) conducted a survey of 877 mainland Chinese participants and found that foreign-language films had greater appeal to younger audiences, many of whom preferred bilingual subtitles. In comparison, dubbing was better received among older adults. A one-size-fits-all translation is, at best, a move *faute de mieux*. With the advent of novel digital reading practices and a globalised information landscape, the way audiences engage with content has been transformed. This evolution poses new challenges for reception researchers, urging us to proceed with responsibility and innovation as we chart new directions.

While some claim that real readers serve as 'the ultimate arbiters of the reception' of a translation (Chen, 2024: 302), it is crucial to keep in mind that readers are neither wholly objective nor entirely within our reach. Kobus Marais (2019: 20) criticises Toury's target-oriented paradigm for committing a conceptual fallacy, arguing that it 'reduces the field of translation to the popular, everyday conception of translation by insisting on translation as being determined by reception'. I, too, would demur at the idea of an all-encompassing, idolised-idealised reader. Nevertheless, Marais's claim that translation scholars overstate the role of reception, rendering translation hostage to public opinion, seems like a false dichotomy.

To study reception is not to surrender to the capricious tides of popular sensibility, but to resist what Marais (2019) terms the 'linguistic bias' that haunts translation studies. More than that, it is an attempt to stand before the untamed, fragmented nature of translation itself, and to acknowledge its dissonances without subduing them and to embrace its irresolvable tensions without forcing them into the brittle scaffolding of order. Reception, after all, is no mere passive absorption but a battleground of ideologies, a restless confluence of perspectives that on occasion refuse to be reconciled.

In our digital, post-truth epoch in which a new technocratic order looms, responses to multilingual and multimodal content grow ever more volatile. If we are to take translation and its implications seriously, we must recognise the ephemeral, insular nature of reader expectations (not as immutable truths but as hypotheses to be tested) as shifting voices in an ongoing and unfinished dialogue. No single agent, including author, translator, client, critic, academic, or reader, can claim absolute authority; instead, reception remains an open-ended negotiation, a timeless and ceaseless navigation of *difference*.

2 User Expectations and Assessment

In this section, I revisit how the fundamental concepts of translation invoke approaches associated with the target reader. In particular, I outline key approaches to constructing a mental model of the recipients and testing user expectations of translations in various genres and modalities. Some ideas are invoked to bolster an argument, while others seek to stir polemical debate.

2.1 What about Heterogeneous Readerships?

A pragmatic perspective is particularly illuminating because it emphasises that the receiver reassuringly plays an essential role in the communication between the mediator (as the secondary sender of the translation) and the final receiver (Padilla et al., 1999). One may argue that the readers of translations can only ever be truly understood in the sociocultural contexts that originally constituted them. Notably, reception studies at the societal level tend to focus on 'theoretical readers', whilst more recent empirical studies have shifted their gaze towards the nuanced experiences of 'real readers'.

When exploring how a text is received, a more pertinent question arises: 'What is the extent to which translational efforts can cater to a diverse group of recipients and to what degree can we provide insights for credible, authentic polyvocality in the reception?' In Chen's (2023) analysis of how different audiences have received two Chinese translations of E.B. White's *Charlotte's Web* (1952), one by Xin Kang in 1979 and another by Rongrong Ren in 2004, she made an interesting comparative case for a divergent translation reception. She argued that although critics have praised Ren's translation for its use of 'colloquialisms', 'humour' and 'childlike language', ordinary readers' opinions on its suitability for children remain divided. Some readers appreciate the accessible, straightforward language for young audiences, whilst others argue that it lacks the qualities necessary for presenting engaging experiences.

The ambiguities surrounding the identity and behaviour of the receiver loom large, challenging and destabilising conventional thinking. Essentially, reception revels in paradoxes, ambiguities, and fluid boundaries, thereby representing a state of indeterminacy that defies rigid categorisation. I do not intend to dwell on these elusive paradoxes for their own sake but rather to view them as a rejection of a universal approach to translation. Here, my contention is to reveal the inherent uncertainties that mark the generic complexities of translational receptions.

In this context, 'readers' can be a broad term that includes the translator (thus serving as the text's first reader) and other agents, including the implied reader, interpretive community, critics, the empirical reader, and the target culture as a whole. In certain cases, the intended recipient of a text is self-evident, and the referent can be readily understood and identified. However, in other genres of discourse, such as literary works, AVTs, or conference interpreting events, audiences are inherently unpredictable or fictitious.

In this vein, Venuti's (2008) argument accords with Chesterman's (1998) classification of typical and atypical readers. Venuti proclaims that in the Anglophone context, especially when translation flows from a minoritised to a majoritised language, the expectations of a certain cadre of professional readers legitimise a set of ideals and practices that demand the complete assimilation of a translation into the recipient culture's linguistic and aesthetic norms. Therefore, such readers expect translations to expunge every trace of the foreign, fulfilling the normative imperative of impeccable fluency. Such a somehow hegemonic, arguably neocolonialist stance implies that a translation's success is gauged by its invisibility; that is, a piece of well-translated text is one that does not appear to be translated at all (Arrojo, 1997).

Illuminating as such classifications may be, one consequence of favouring readers is reconfiguring the reception, which emerges as a kind of hybrid. The reception of children's literature is a good example. This peculiar genre includes texts deemed appropriate for children not only by their creators, such as authors and publishers, but also by key figures in the literary marketplace and educational institutions, including critics, school teachers and librarians (O'Sullivan, 2012). Intriguingly, readers do not always conform to neat moulds; that said, paradoxically, children are not the sole target audience for children's literature. Adults also engage with these texts, whether for personal enjoyment, shared reading experiences with children, or to oversee the content and ensure it is age-appropriate (Alvstad, 2010: 24). Such a dual readership engenders a unique dynamic characterised by the 'unequal relationship that arises from the assignment of texts by adults to children' (O'Sullivan, 2012: 452). Nevertheless, aside from studies that use adult reactions merely as a benchmark against child readers' responses, research on the reception of translated children's literature by adults remains notably sparse (see, e.g. H. Kruger, 2013). Given the multiplicity of readerships spanning professional and general audiences, children and adults, and source text and target text readers, findings in this area are far from monolithic.

A good line of empirical studies has attempted to compare the reception of translations among different readers, such as professional and general readers, in journalistic translation (Chen, 2011; Eker Roditakis, 2017). Others, notably Liu and Baer (2017), have sought to demonstrate how literary translations resonate with nonspecialist readers, thereby revealing the delicate engagement between the text and the untrained eye. Professional readers, such as reviewers, arguably play a decisive role as influential mediators with the power to consecrate foreign authors and significantly impact the reception and prestige of translated texts (Eker Roditakis, 2017).

At times, the boundaries that distinguish between different types of readers shift and are crossed, reminding us that readers resist reductive categorisation such that even 'general readers' may also assume the roles of critic and translator. In Chan's (2010) study, fan-readers entertained themselves by reviewing translations, with some even forming online communities to undertake translations on their own. Similarly, Chen's (2024) work melds book reviews of literary critics with the online musings of general readers, echoing Batchelor's (2018: 157–158) notion of 'audience-created' paratexts. Through an analysis of blogs and media platforms, Işıklar Koçak (2017) found that online readers are as discerning as translators and publishers when it comes to criteria for selecting retranslations. Whilst these standards provide a reference point, reader responses vary. This notion is evidenced by Demirkol Ertürk's (2024) discussion of online responses to two English translations of a seminal twentieth-century Turkish novel in which the perspectives of online readers differ markedly from those of publishers and critics.

This variation unveils the inherent nature of reader expectations, which is cluttered and palimpsestic. Preconceived notions about translation strategies can transform how readers engage with a text, thus reshaping their assumptions and even redefining what counts as translation. Given the inherent heterogeneity of audiences, it is misleading to speak of a 'unitary' interpretive community (Lindlof et al., 1998: 242).

Pioneering research in interpreting (e.g. Kurz, 1993) has revealed divergent expectation patterns among different user groups, including doctors, engineers, and international delegates, pointing to the fact that domain-specific preferences play a significant role. Notably, Kurz and Pöchhacker (1995) discovered that German-speaking TV anchors and programme heads prioritised fluid delivery and a pleasing vocal quality over strict completeness, the latter of which is a criterion traditionally deemed essential in interpreting.

Moreover, empirical studies have demonstrated that extralinguistic factors, such as nonsyntactic pauses and monotonous intonation (Lenglet & Michaux, 2020) as well as nonnative accents (Cheung, 2013), significantly influence user perceptions. Perhaps more interesting, research on user expectations in interpreting has unveiled a clear hierarchy of preferences. In particular, listeners generally favour content-related qualities, including sense consistency, logical cohesion, fluency, and accurate terminology, over delivery features, such as lively intonation, a pleasant voice, and a native accent (Pöchhacker, 2015).

However, due to methodological constraints and substantial variability across studies, our current understanding of these expectations offers only limited, specific guidance for interpreters making decisions in situ. This challenge is even more pronounced in other communicative settings in which expectations can vary significantly by domain, country, and even organisation. Pöchhacker (2015) also underlines the variability of user preferences, noting that factors such as meeting size, technical specificity, age, gender, and conference experience all influence expectations. At the same time, the various taxonomies, classifications, and distinctions of readerships may be too simplistic to do justice to the complexity of translation reception as a socio-cognitive phenomenon or experience. Thus, moving beyond any analysis of individual moments of reception, we need a method for generalising expectations and acknowledging idiosyncrasy.

2.2 Expectancy Norms and Socio-cognitive Templates

Expectations, broadly understood as personal anticipations of what one is likely or desirous to receive, are essential for evaluating the quality and efficacy of any activity. As reflections of an individual's perspective on events mediated by external agents, expectations are bound to change and constantly evolve over time.

The exploration of readers' expectations dates back to Jauss's formulation of the aesthetic of reception (*Rezeptionsaesthetik*), which debunks all established authority of a text's 'original' meaning of production. Jauss introduced the term 'horizon of expectations' (*Erwartungshorizont*) as a desire to describe the cultural enquiries, assumptions, and evaluative criteria that inform how readers interpret and assess literary works within specific historical contexts. This proposition reflects American theorist Stanley Fish's assertion that a reader's role constructs the meaning of the text itself. For Fish (1980), a text's meaning emerges only within its readers' own cultural references and assumptions. This notion is also compatible with Gadamer (1975: 336), who takes an even broader view of the historical finiteness of our being: 'After us, others will understand in a different way.' This idea extends the so-called 'horizon of expectations' beyond individual subjectivity, anchoring it in collective factors (e.g. history, geography, social status, education, age, and gender) and imbuing the concept of reception with broader sociocultural and political dispensation.

Reader expectations, however, inevitably evoke the spectre of contingency because they are patently idiosyncratic. A commonly voiced complaint is that no two readers will resemble one another even remotely. In their attempt to map out shared grounds in translation, Kotze et al. (2021) conceived expectancy norms as socio-cognitive constructs that function as mental 'templates' developed by readers through socialisation. In this sense, translation norms are understood as socio-cognitive constructs; that is, mental 'templates' developed through socialisation that guide individuals in their conceptualisations, evaluations, and responses to translations. These norms influence translation decision-making both as rational constructs for evaluation and as experiential, affective phenomena (Halverson & Kotze, 2022; Robinson, 2020). Furthermore, rooted in socioculturally shared knowledge, these templates call forth vivid mental scenes that direct readers' (albeit often idealised) perceptions, evaluations, and responses to translations, ultimately steering their behaviours.

The referenced study by Kotze et al. (2021) explores the normative constructs and cognitive-evaluative templates that readers adopt to rationalise, assess, and engage with translated texts. Here, the template is reconfigured as a structured assemblage of parameters that guide the perception and evaluation of translation, thereby emerging from discernible patterns within users' narratives on the subject. As a working hypothesis, such a template offers us an exploratory model for thinking through the ambiguities of reception, encapsulating a composite of normative perspectives on translation.

Thus far, past studies have proposed constructive attempts to empirically contextualise how various forms of socio-cognitive 'templates' of expectations impact translation reception. As discussed, one intriguing hypothesis posits that childhood nostalgia, as a form of collective and cultural memory that extends beyond individual recollections of past experiences, may influence the reception of translated children's literature. Given the unique role of children's literature in evoking feelings of childhood nostalgia (Santesso, 2006), a nostalgic mindset may influence how translated children's books are consumed as cultural artefacts, a hermeneutic of reception and allegorisation. As individuals grow older, some retain fond memories of the translations they read in their youth and seek to revisit these familiar texts, even when newer translations are available. Drawing on the concept of 'nostalgic consumption', Chen (2023) theorised that this nostalgia accounts for why certain adult readers display a preference for older translations that they encountered as children and recalled as memorable. This nostalgic mentality, termed the reader's 'reminiscence bump' (Pillemer, 2001: 125), can also indicate why translated children's literature is cherished not merely as text but as a representation of timeless cultural appeal.

Another example of a socio-cognitive template is Yang's (2023) application of the parasocial interaction framework (PSI; Horton & Wohl, 1956) using *danmu* comments on a specific interpreter-mediated event as a case study. In particular, PSI invokes the importance of examining how viewers engage with media personas. In accordance with this framework, cognitive responses arise through various processes, including the mindful allocation of attention, a nuanced grasp of a persona's actions informed by previous media and life experiences, the critical appraisal of that persona, and the forging of relationships between the persona and the viewer. By focusing on cognitive and affective responses, Yang (2023) analyses how these processes manifest in real-time verbal interactions on the *danmu* platform. The so-called cognitive responses include viewers' perceptions, evaluations, and personal associations with the media persona, whilst affective responses pertain to emotional reactions, such as empathy or sympathy. Given that *danmu* comments capture immediate, context-driven reactions, they serve as direct expressions of users' cognitive and emotional processes. By linking users' verbal reactions to underlying psychological processes, the study adds to our understanding of interpreting audiences' interactions with media personas, thus contributing to a better comprehension of parasocial engagement in digital contexts (Yang, 2023). For Yang, the PSI template facilitates a systematic examination of the diverse range of reactions expressed in *danmu*, offering a structured approach to deciphering them. In addition, the template allows for the extraction of relevant responses from the otherwise chaotic nature of the online social site, which is custom-designed for a post-democratic age.

In terms of working methods and theoretical accounts, imagology, as the discursive articulations of national, cultural, or ethnic characterisations, can also be considered broader mental images or representations of national character and serve as another plausible socio-cognitive template for translation reception. Rather than investigating identities or what nations inherently 'are', imagology offers a rhizomatic epistemological model for understanding how they are discursively constructed and reshaped within target cultures. Thus, through self-, hetero- and meta-image constructions, imagology aims to reveal the applications of national characterisation and the underlying mechanisms of national stereotyping. One example comes from Li's (2018) attempt to describe the images conveyed or crafted through translational activities, including text selection, translation, introduction, interpretation, and reception.

Viewed from another perspective, socio-cognitive templates are, at best, falsifiable hypotheses with an essentially heuristic role and thus serve as guideposts for empirical testing. As we explore the relevance, adaptability, and potential of reader-centred concepts, we expand them beyond a singular dimension into epistemological awareness at the metacognitive level. In this process, we acknowledge that, too often, readers are expected to be plagued by various expectations that coexist or conflict with each other. For instance, in the case of the nostalgic template, an important proviso is that childhood memories fade, and erroneous conceptions of the translation mingle with varying translation norms and traditions. A nostalgic account may, nevertheless, simplify and gloss over other embedded contexts of the text. We may wonder how social contexts sit alongside readers' collective memories or how cultural memories of literary preference are supposed to work.

Expectation is not a monolithic construct, but rather a collision of conflicts and discontinuity. The manner in which readers internalise, reinforce, and balance these expectancy templates has received scant attention, with few exceptions (e.g. Valdez, 2023). After all, one may say that these templates function as a kind of neo-Kantian idealism, poised for empirical exploration into the relationship between the mental representations of audiences, their anticipated reactions, and the responses they ultimately exhibit.

2.3 User Expectations and Audience Design

The user-oriented paradigm, as an emerging reception-focused research line, brings user expectations to the fore by openly regarding interpretative quality and actual comprehension within defined contextual frameworks. This body of research predominantly uses survey methodologies whilst integrating experimental approaches to a limited degree. From the perspective of interpreting, Pöchhacker (2015: 430) posits that 'expectations' are 'beliefs about what one is likely to get, or would like to get', suggesting that a normative model of excellence when interpreting is viewed as a service for *users*. Pöchhacker's idea includes both receivers' anticipation of what they 'would' have received and their ideals of what they 'ought to' receive; in this case, 'would' often transforms into 'should'. In exploring what the 'ought to' component entails, quality expectations are understood as internalising 'expectancy norms' (Chesterman, 1993). Serving as a useful conceptual frame of reference, the term is understood as an 'ideal standard' of performance, one that is anchored in prior experience (Teas, 1993: 18) as well as transcends and defies the reader's expectations.

The foregoing adumbration of the definition, as navigated by user expectations, would remain unfair without acknowledging its paramount role in performance assessment, a significance vividly demonstrated in survey research on interpreting studies. Some scholars have posited that optimal interpreting quality is attained when interpreters successfully meet, or even exceed, these expectations (see Russo, 2005; René de Cotret et al., 2021). Pöchhacker's position implies that interpreting quality is a rather subjective assessment. To him, 'the degree of 'success', or indeed any other quality criterion, is necessarily judged from a particular (subjective) perspective in and on the communicative event' (Pöchhacker, 2002: 97), including those of professional peers, clients or listeners.

At this point, a full exegesis of how interpreting quality is configured by user expectations would divert us too far from our main foci. Suffice it to say that interpreting quality is inherently situational: It is judged in light of the specific contexts in which it is produced, grounded in diverse user perspectives (Angelelli, 2004). Reflecting on the fluidity of expectations amid sociocultural, political, economic, and pragmatic tensions, Garzone (2002: 107) observed that 'quality is the sum of several different, heterogeneous aspects'. In other words, as interpreters, speakers, receivers, and end-user clients each bring their own distinct views to bear, quality expectations inevitably vary. Referring to legal interpreting, Hale (2006: 220) accedes to the observation that interpreters are typically entangled in the crosscurrents of divergent expectations, often 'feeling pressured' by various stakeholders and confronted with the challenge of navigating conflicting identities.

Given the multiplicity of perspectives and the varied roles of users, empirical investigations into user expectations have frequently relied on surveys to explore how interpreters are perceived, especially in specialised settings. This tradition can be traced back to the nascent days of interpreting studies, when Bühler's seminal survey (1986) marked the first attempt to capture the opinions of high-profile AIIC conference interpreters, in which 16 sets of linguistic and extralinguistic quality criteria were rated. Such a research line traditionally targets professional interpreters. Such a focus, as critics have argued, neglects the genuine users of interpreting services. Bühler's top-down criteria, derived from accreditation standards, ethical codes, and professional guidelines, were designed with service end users in mind. Notably, this initial foray merely served as a launching pad, and subsequent studies have expanded the user base to include TV hosts (Kurz & Pöchhacker, 1995), legal experts

(Christensen, 2011; Collados Aís et al., 2007; Pérez-Luzardo Díaz, 2015), film critics (Russo, 2005), and community members (Kaczmarek, 2016).

Using Bühler's criteria as the ideal benchmark, Kurz's (1993) survey revealed that conference participants, by and large, proved less exacting than the professional interpreters in Bühler's study. Bühler herself noted this methodological issue, emphasising the need to 'differentiate between expectations, that might not always be realistic, and actual needs' (1986: 231). Indeed, surveying different stakeholders' perceptions in accordance with their desires and opinions reveals a mixed view of expectations. For example, Hale's (2007) study of twenty-one Australian lawyers revealed that most participants prioritised accuracy, specifically the faithful rendering of the original, as the core criterion for interpreting. Notably, Kelly (2000) identified mixed views on interpreters' cultural mediation responsibilities, concluding that more than half of judges and nearly half of prosecutors considered this beyond the interpreter's role. Hale (2004) further suggested that laypersons were less concerned with interpreters' cultural responsibilities and more with their role of serving as translating machines. Collectively, these studies have claimed certain kinds of continuity between user expectations while highlighting the diversity of expectations across different roles. On the one hand, some groups viewed interpreters as cultural mediators; on the other hand, others viewed them as neutral, if not mechanical, linguistic intermediaries. In this sense, expectations are squarely caught between identities.

In addition, the limited comparability of surveys in user expectation research is pronounced. The normative expectations used in surveys can cause terminological confusion. For example, as Bühler (1986: 234) diagnosed, 'The formulation of some criteria gave rise to misunderstandings.' Pöchhacker (2015) further noted that certain criteria, such as 'completeness', may ring true for some but hold varied meanings for other respondents, highlighting ambiguities and potential overlaps in the criteria. In scenarios that lack contextual grounding, items such as 'use of appropriate style' remain ambiguous and ill-defined, whilst others such as 'sense consistency with original message' and 'completeness of interpretation' are challenging for one-site, monolingual users to evaluate directly. This is a limitation to which Bühler (1986) herself was always attuned. By the same token, Pérez-Luzardo Díaz (2015) questioned the criterion of 'use of appropriate style', highlighting the subjective and variable definitions of 'style' used in some survey studies. Liu (2023) astutely identified a key limitation in Bühler's typology, noting that it did not clearly distinguish between the expectations of interpreters and those of users. In this sense, an exclusively interpreter-centric pursuit of user expectations becomes almost a terminological anomaly.

This raises another pertinent question about the hierarchy of users. In accordance with classical audience design theory, a text that outlives the author can be interpreted in three ways: as directed towards a specific referent, towards an imagined audience, or intended for strangers (Bell, 1984; Mason, 2000). The dynamic hierarchy of readerships provides insights into how interpreters can translate effectively to achieve maximum communicative impact. In this context, failure to address the primary audience carries the highest risk of communicative failure or credibility loss – optimistic but within reach. Nevertheless, I would submit that disregarding more distant readers and failing to consider the long-term implications of translation could result in unethical outcomes, such as reader distrust stemming from translator manipulation (Hu, 2022). Perceived distortion and manipulation appear to be anathema to readers' acceptance of a text. What is at stake is to remain open to the ambiguity, paradox, and tension in users' expectations alongside the discernment that to resist the impulse can help harmonise apparently conflicting values in reception.

Although user expectations are sociocultural and ideologically influenced, research on reception has predominantly been associated with textual models of analysis. What this obscures, however, are extralinguistic criteria like trust, emotion, behavioural change, and actionability. An exception to this reluctance to affective response is the study of Rojo, Ramos, and Valenzuela (2014), who investigated how metaphorical versus nonmetaphorical translations of figurative expressions affect readers' emotional responses, as measured by heart rate. In particular, they discovered that metaphorical translations provoke markedly heightened emotional responses, whether sorrow, fury, terror, or joy, suggesting that translation strategies wield a direct influence over readers' emotional engagement and draw them into narrative worlds.

This finding corresponds to audience immersion as a kind of cognitive expectation, which has gained notable traction within the realm of AVT (see also Brems & Pinto, 2013). A rich line of research has tapped into diverse topics, from the allocation of attention and reading behaviours to the subtleties of subtitling conventions and their profound influences on cognitive mechanisms and immersion. Studies have also found that factors such as reading habits (Krejtz et al., 2013), presentation speed (Romero-Fresco, 2015; Szarkowska et al., 2011), and a reader's own linguistic schema and language proficiency (Kruger, 2013, 2016) all play crucial roles in current debates about how dynamic texts are received. At its core, the contentious issue remains that the reader, and indeed, human cognition, is the principal subject of reading research, whilst translation itself evolves as an experimental form in terms of content and structure. In this light, reception emerges as a distinctly cognitive human act, which integrates planning, reflection, decision-making, and emotional response, in tandem with process-oriented studies in cognitive translation (Jakobsen, 2017; Jakobsen & Alves, 2020).

2.4 From Usability to Accessibility

Grounded in usability studies and indebted to the pragmatism espoused by functionalism, some translation researchers advocate the iterative integration of user response data into the translation process to enhance user friendliness. Suojanen, Koskinen, and Tuominen (2015) argued for a user-centred approach to translation. Whilst this paradigm operationalises key concepts from functionalist translation theories by providing translators with empirical insights into actual readers' needs and preferences, the focus is notably distinct. Earlier target-side functionalists, such as Nord (2001), placed greater emphasis on the importance of ensuring a client's briefs (*Auftrag*) were as detailed as possible, especially when the final decision rests with the client. In an interesting passage, Nord asserts that '[t]he translation purpose is defined by the translation brief' (2001: 201), serving as 'the ideal of the commercial skopos', as Newmark (1997: 75) slightly ironically put it. In this case, the functionalist's simplistic understanding of reception as accepting a client's word as truth seems like a proverbial low-hanging fruit.

Taking a different point of departure, the user-centred translation model champions the continuous collection of user data generated from the translation process. This process-driven paradigm enables translators to cultivate a refined understanding of the end user and optimise translations for maximum usability. Furthermore, usability models have become indispensable, especially in highly professional fields such as AVT, in which the user experience is the ultimate benchmark. Drawing on the insights of psychological immersion, usability studies, and cognitive load theories, this approach underlines the dynamics between verbal content, non-verbal stimuli and auditory cues, thereby shaping the reception of polysemiotic narratives (Suojanen et al., 2015).

Another point echoing pragmatism is that, for usability proponents, this form of collected target-side information is mainly to inform the production process, effectively linking quality assessment to the user experience. In support of this view, Wehrmeyer (2014: 376) explicitly argues that a reception-oriented focus on translation must incorporate the target receiver into its evaluative framework. From a usage-based perspective, H. Kruger (2016) draws on Venuti's (2008) distinctions of fluency versus resistance (i.e. domestication versus foreignisation) to contend that the discursive markers of 'fluency' or 'resistance' must be examined through the lens of individual cognitive processing. Such analysis is essential for understanding how translations in their dynamic interaction with reader cognition, exert either domesticating or foreignising influences on society at large. This is a fair point whose primary aim is pragmatic: Usability research integrates actual user responses with the aim of transcending individual idiosyncratic expectations to address broader societal applications and implications as much as possible.

Partly propelled by the advent of accessibility laws, including the Americans with Disabilities Act and the EU Audiovisual Media Services Directive, as also exemplified by European e-Inclusion and e-Accessibility policies, the usability approach to translation reception prompts us to reconsider our collective response to ethical challenges. Here, the concept of '(media) accessibility' presents a remarkable advancement in technology-enabled translation training and practices, integrating broader concepts such as creativity, technological literacy, and social inclusion, particularly in the AVT context. Furthermore, this concept prompts translators to consider diverse contextual factors and technical constraints, often with a focus on users with special needs (Greco, 2018; Romero-Fresco & Dangerfield, 2022).

Recent scholarship has examined accessibility practices, including subtitling for the D/deaf and hard-of-hearing (Zárate, 2021), automatic speech recognition technologies, such as respeaking and live subtitling, and audio descriptions for vulnerable communities with sensory impairments (Romero-Fresco & Pöchhacker, 2017). The concept of 'accessibility' has now expanded beyond impairments, as Mazur and Vercauteren (2019) advocated, equally focusing on the diverse communicative channels in audio-visual production, thus making translated media accessible to a broad spectrum of users. Identifying the boom of (media) accessibility to the moment when technology transformed the reading experience for translators and users alike, one may also consider accessibility as a pursuit of a more democratic and egalitarian social order that is compatible with the following statement: '[T]ranslation is increasingly revealed as the means to create fair conditions for language minorities to *access* their human rights' (Monzó-Nebot & Mellinger, 2022, emphasis mine).

Empirical models of translation reception, which assess quality, usability, and accessibility by looking into the effects of translations on readers, represent a societal realisation of functionalist theories that emphasise target-culture orientation and acceptability. Be that as it may, these proposals, still in their early boom stages within the research agenda, invite further explorations and thoughtful refinements. Specifically, in the realm of written translation, only a few evidence-based studies have demonstrated how reader responses to translations can inform translators' mental models of their target audiences, and how this, in turn, could influence translation processes. Some attempts will be examined on methodological grounds in the following section.

3 Approaches to Testing Reception in High-Stakes Communication

Drawing on a series of empirical examples, this section examines prevailing and innovative research methods that are designed to assess reader comprehension alongside the acceptability and actionability of multimodal texts. Beyond cataloguing methodologies, this section offers illustrations and critical comparisons that reveal the promise and pitfalls of different approaches. The section aims to ask larger, more fundamental questions: What does it mean to study translation reception across cultures? How do we study not just language but experience, cognition, and perception? How is reception both personal and governed by collective memory, historical constraints, and social conventions? Whether tracked through survey responses, big data analytics, or eye movements, the essence of translation reception does not change but remains what it has always been: the other side of a dialogue. What shifts is our perspective on the process in terms of how we see and study it, allowing us to understand it anew.

3.1 From Questionnaire Surveys to Naturalistic Observations

Interviews and questionnaires have long served as indispensable tools in reception studies, enabling researchers to investigate reader assessment, comprehension, and satisfaction, not just in what they understand but in what lingers, what resists, and what quietly reshapes their perceptions. In other words, these methods reveal the confluence between expectations and interpretations. Questionnaires, in particular, have been widely used to explore how readers' cultural background, language proficiency, and social affiliations determine their evaluation of translated texts. When thoughtfully designed, surveys can provide quantitative data and yield insights into the dynamics of dependent variables, thus allowing for the empirical testing of hypotheses on reader engagement and textual reception.

A pioneering example must be mentioned here. Puurtinen (1994) devised an experiment that integrated three distinct approaches: a comprehension test with children, a reading-aloud assessment with teachers, and subjective evaluations by translation students. Her focus was on the stylistic ways in which two Finnish translations of *The Wizard of Oz* influenced, or perhaps unsettled, readers' experiences. The tension between domestication and foreignisation, or between the comfort of the known and the pull of the unfamiliar, is at the centre of Liang's (2007) work on Taiwanese readers and the Harry Potter series. His study did not simply measure preference, as it also illustrated a quiet resistance in which readers connoted the rejection of foreignised lexical choices, as if certain words, which were too distant and too strange, could break the spell of immersion itself.

In recent years, reception studies have gone beyond the realm of literature into unexpected corners. For instance, surveys have offered a rare glimpse into the lives of church interpreters, including their motivations as well as their positioning in communities where faith and language are inseparable (Downie, 2024). Studies by Valero-Garcés (2022) and Mężyk (2022) have shown how interpretations in Spanish and Polish churches are influenced by recruitment practices, role expectations, and the quiet, persistent work of volunteers.

While survey-based studies on user expectations offer various attractions and virtues, several methodological shortcomings and blind spots can be identified, complicating the very conclusions they seek to draw. In the context of interpreting studies, Moser (1996: 157) lamented that survey results are often reflections of the users themselves. Such reflections are defined by users' own characteristics, biases, and experiences, making it difficult to extract a broader, more universal measure of reception. This lack of shared understanding extends beyond survey respondents and seeps into the very research that builds upon these studies, thereby leading to disparate interpretations among scholars working with ostensibly similar constructs. The result? A fractured landscape of user expectation analysis in which consistency in assessing varied variables is lacking.

For example, following Bühler's (1986) seminal work on user expectations, subsequent scholars have sought to impose a top-down framework to systematise these shifting perceptions. Kurz (1993) and Moser (1996) explored user evaluations, while Zwischenberger (2013) examined the effects of these subjective perceptions on diverse user groups. Efforts to categorise reception-based quality assessments also emerged (Garzone, 2002), but these attempts were constrained by constructs that remained underdeveloped. Such constructs included quality criteria that were individually defined and conceptually overlapping, inconsistent in format, and statistically imprecise, a problem for which Pöchhacker (2005) provided in-depth elaboration.

Even in the analysis of the survey data, interpretation remains fraught with pitfalls and fallacies. Pöchhacker (2005) underlined misplaced criticisms directed at Bühler (1986). Contrary to detractors, Bühler had correctly used percentages rather than means when handling ordinal data. The problem, he argued, is fundamental: Means assume equal score intervals, a flawed premise for ordinal data in which the mode and median serve as more appropriate measures (Stevens, 1946). Liu (2023) proposed a corrective approach and advocated for the joint use of multipoint rating scales and rank-ordering methods to paint a fuller picture of user perception. While scales capture the intensity of perception, rank-ordering clarifies relative importance, thus allowing researchers to move beyond isolated scores and into comparative reception analysis. Frequencies (e.g. counts and percentages) remain the backbone of ordinal data representation. Nevertheless, incorporating measures of central tendency, such as mode and median, enhances comparability across studies, making reception survey results less fragmented and more interpretable.

Calls have been persistent for the use of a standardised questionnaire framework in reception studies, with scholars advocating for models that balance consistency with adaptability and allow for context-specific modifications (e.g. church interpreting in Downie, 2024). The like-minded notion of survey data harmonisation, championed by Mack and Cattaruzza (1995), has been widely adopted in broader social sciences (Slomczynski et al., 2024) but has gained limited traction in translation and interpreting studies. Its successful application elsewhere points to an unexplored, but promising, frontier.

However, while user surveys have long operated within predetermined parameters, whether we have fully tapped into users' interpretive and analytical potential remains elusive. The premise is rather clear: User expectations are often half told, sometimes contradictory, mired in contingency, and pose challenges for researchers seeking to identify patterns of collective behaviour that may be difficult, if not impossible, to generalise. The top-down structure of questionnaires may flatten reception, providing only a partial picture of user perceptions, and call for supplementary bottom-up methodologies. In response, post hoc measures, such as comprehension tests, interviews, semantic profiling, and association tasks, are increasingly used along with surveys, allowing for a dialectical interplay between quantitative and qualitative strands that converge and redefine each other.

One such approach entails incorporating an open-ended-question phase into the design, in which preliminary findings function not as definitive conclusions but as starting points for qualitative enquiries (e.g. Li, 2024; Wehrmeyer, 2014). When combined with follow-up interviews (Ameri & Khoshsaligheh, 2020; Briechle & Eppler, 2019; Hu, 2022), this integrated approach yields a more spontaneous, descriptive, and exploratory understanding of reception, which is less constrained by preset categories and more attuned to the actual experiences of translation users.

The rise of (pseudo-)experimental methodologies has reshaped how researchers approach reader expectations, moving beyond passive observation to controlled recontextualisation. No longer confined to retrospective judgements, reception studies have increasingly turned towards an 'experimental user response paradigm' (Pöchhacker, 2018: 263), in which reception can thus be viewed as an active engagement. This is exemplified in Valdez et al.'s (2025) recent study, which adopts a multi-method, reception-oriented approach to examine how translated vaccination-related public health information is processed by readers. The study combines three methodological components: participant-paced, region-by-region reading to track real-time reading patterns; an incremental judgment task where participants indicate when the text stops making sense; and a post-reading comprehension questionnaire. The triangulated data confirmed that reading difficulties and misinterpretations were not limited to non-native readers and were often linked to complex medical language. Another illuminating example comes from Cheung (2022), whose experiment examined how listeners' reliance on simultaneous interpreting affected their perceptions of its quality. His findings suggest a serious compromise between user expectations: In on-site settings, the greater the users' dependence on interpreting, the higher their quality assessment tends to be, regardless of how non-native an interpreter's accent may seem. This finding, which suggests that user expectations are not static absolutes but conditioned, represents an instrumentalist stance in which users' prior experiences and pragmatic demands intertwine (Sternberg & Sternberg, 2016).

Another strand of user expectation research gathers user perceptions in real time immediately after observing a performance, thus reducing the risk of treating quality as merely normative rather than context-specific. Consequently, users' responses likely reflect their experiences and the actual criteria they use to assess performance in specific settings. In a recent study, Yang (2023) examined user reception of interpreting events through real-time engagement and investigated video users' parasocial interactions with a specific interpreter on a *danmu* interface. Using the public hearing of Chinese athlete Sun Yang, interpreted ad hoc on the Chinese video-sharing platform BiliBili as a case study, Yang demonstrated how audience reception is far from a neutral assessment of linguistic competence but is instead entangled in social and ideological currents. In this example, immediate public feedback refracts from national sentiment, collective empathy, and broader political undercurrents, particularly in the case of a high-profile Chinese athlete being subjected to external scrutiny. Here, the reception of interpreting becomes a contested situation in which identity and power intersect, factors that are shaped as much by nationalist sentiment as by any technical standard of interpreting performance. The participatory nature of digital platforms further amplifies this dynamic, revealing shifting narratives about the profession of interpreting and the ways in which its role and credibility are continuously negotiated.

With the boom of translation technologies, another line of survey enquiry emerged, specifically exploring how user experience relates to technology-mediated scenarios. Investigating a sample of 1,200 participants in the United

Kingdom, Vieira et al. (2023) found that the participants had used machine translation in their daily lives, most with satisfaction, thereby indicating that (machine) translation has become a routine social activity in recent years. Furthermore, Braun (2018) examined the use of video-mediated interpreting (VMI) in legal proceedings while considering sociopolitical factors influencing its development in the profession, thus providing a comparative analysis of interpreter perceptions of VMI across multiple countries, settings, and configurations.

However, a persistent challenge remains: Stated user expectations often fail to align with the assessment criteria used in actual practice (Collados Aís, 2002; Garzone, 2002). This means that the standards dismissed by users as ideologically nonessential may somehow influence their evaluations in actual practice. As suggested by Kalina (2004), first impressions, biases, and emotions, including stereotypes, play a crucial role in shaping quality preferences (Garzone, 2002; Grbić, 2008). In this light, Liu (2023) criticised the lack of methodological rigour in some user-based research and advocated for the stronger incorporation of users' actual experiences to ensure more empirically testable findings. After all, subjective opinions are the products of our culture.

One way forward, as Liu (2023: 62) suggested, is the use of a 'two-pronged approach', which examines user attitudes and behaviours to understand how specific attributes of translation and interpreting influence preferences and satisfaction. From an onomasiological perspective, Liu recommended that the field move towards the more experientially grounded term 'user experience research', thus aligning reception studies with the practical concerns of usability research. Such user research has been particularly impactful in accessibility, in which reception research is not necessarily viewed as a purely academic pursuit but has an ethical imperative. Experimental designs tailored to audiences with sensory impairments help ensure that translation, interpreting, and accessibility efforts are construed by cognitive realities rather than speculation. In Xiao et al. (2015), participants engaged in sign language-mediated content followed by comprehension tests, resulting in a study that offers empirical grounding for user-centred design and accessibility policies.

At stake is not just a methodological shift but an epistemological one; that is, peeling back the layers of reception as it emerges in real-world scenarios. Christensen's (2011) study exemplifies this notion, combining case-based surveys, transcript analysis, documentary examination, and on-site observations together to trace the often unspoken alignment (or misalignment) between user expectations and the interpreter's self-perception within the charged space of a Danish courtroom. Ethnographic approaches, such as that proposed by Tekgül (2019), push this idea further, opting for the unobtrusive, the ambient, and the organic. Instead of extracting responses in sterile conditions, these studies follow readers in their natural environments, capturing how they talk about texts and situate translations within broader social and institutional frames. However, like all methodologies, ethnographic work is not immune to criticism; rather, it remains situational, context-specific, and resistant to broad generalisation.

Beyond testing reception in naturalistic settings, another somewhat balanced approach lies in comparative judgement, in which participants are asked to rank and assess multiple translations of the same source text that reflect varying degrees of translator intervention in a quasi-experiential setting. This method does not frame reception as a binary choice between better and worse; instead, it represents a process of weighing competing strategies in which readers must navigate trade-offs, contingencies, and interpretive risks (Hu, 2020, 2022; Pym & K. Hu, 2025).

Notably, comparative evaluations by actual users in a controlled environment, by their very nature, remain a coarse-grained measure. After all, behaviourist methodologies are designed to capture instinctive, unfiltered responses, and such a goal is best achieved when participants are unaware of the experiment's intent (Davies, 2015; Mellinger & Hanson 2022). The more self-conscious the participant, the more the act of assessment alters the very reception it seeks to measure, thus raising critical questions about the uneasy balance between cognitive autonomy and methodological control.

My contention here is that every (reception) approach carries the risk of researcher bias, which represents the imprint of subjective judgement and the subtle weight of prior assumptions shaping outcomes. However, reception itself is not a single, stable entity to be pinned down; it is plural, ever-shifting, and dependent on who is looking, from where, and under what conditions. Rather than seeking one definitive method too quickly, one may concur with heterogeneity: an acceptance of fragmentation, an openness to methodological triangulation, and a willingness to let reception remain unsettled in an empirical sense.

This ethos, which privileges difference, individuality, and self-reflexivity, has given rise to what one may call the 'diversity of unity'. By cross-validating and contrasting multiple methods, triangulation does not erase bias but mitigates it, allowing *new* insights to emerge not from a single vantage point but even from conflicting views. As Whitehead (1967: 244) reminds us, 'It is more important that a proposition be interesting than that it be true.' Perhaps this is the guiding paradox of reception studies: a trial-and-error, falsifiable research paradigm capable of acknowledging that at the centre of every investigation lies not just an objective enquiry, but the inescapable subjectivity of human curiosity itself.

What we seek to measure is never just reception as it exists but rather reception as it is experienced and then refracted through the lens of context, expectation, and the trade-off decision itself.

3.2 Experimental Eye-Tracking Paradigms in Cognition Research

For decades, empirical reception studies have relied on introspective reports, but the past decade has seen an undeniable shift towards the physiological. Psycholinguistic investigations now grapple with questions once considered intangible: How do readers' minds negotiate meaning? Recent technological strides have reshaped the very contours of how we investigate cognitive engagement with translation. Cognitive methodologies now allow researchers to trace the flickers of attention, the speed of reading, and the embodied cognition at play when individuals process translated content. Eye tracking and related biometric tools, once peripheral, have become central instruments in exploring how audiences engage with translation, not merely in theory but also in real time (Walker & Federici, 2018). When paired with experimental or quasi-experimental designs, these techniques allow researchers to move beyond broad assumptions and into the micro-level realities of language processing, immersion, and cognitive load.

Drawing on reading research and experimental paradigms, empirical enquiry in translation reception has increasingly ventured beyond predictable user expectations, turning towards the moment-to-moment processing of multilingual content. Some of the most revelatory works, particularly in audio-visual settings, have used eye-tracking and neuroimaging technologies to capture the imperceptible but consequential ways viewers process subtitles. A significant impetus for using eye-tracking techniques is their ability to capture the cognitive processes underlying the act of reading. Thus, such methods provide crucial insights into attention allocation and reading behaviours (Whyatt et al., 2024). Grounded in the eye–mind assumption (Just & Carpenter, 1980), eye-tracking analysis examines fixation counts, fixation durations, and saccade patterns to elucidate how individuals process multimodal translated content.

This line of online measurements of language processing has developed in tandem with a growing body of behavioural studies, thereby constructing an intricate portrait of reception through experimental rigour and cognitive insight. In place of top-down assumptions, researchers now fine-tune their methodologies to let the data speak, crafting controlled viewing sessions in which cognition itself becomes the subject of enquiry (Kruger, 2016). To offer one pertinent example, Szarkowska et al.'s (2024) investigation into the cognitive friction between dialogue and intralingual subtitles thoroughly examines the very nature of linguistic incongruence and its perceptual consequences. Their mixed methods approach pairs quantitative post-test questionnaires that gauge cognitive load, enjoyment, and comprehension with qualitative insights drawn from semi-structured interviews.

In the realm of static reading, H. Kruger's (2012, 2013) studies represent early attempts to construct a quasi-experimental framework that fuses eye-tracking technology with comprehension and attitude assessments. In particular, these studies investigate the cognitive processing of child and adult Afrikaans readers as they respond to culturally embedded elements in translation. Her study featured a controlled linguistic experiment in which translations of two picture-book pages, each presented in domesticated and foreignised versions, were manipulated. Through a meticulous analysis of eye-tracking metrics, Kruger examined whether different translation strategies left distinct imprints on reading behaviours. The findings revealed a sharp cognitive divergence: Foreignised versions, laden with culturally unfamiliar lexical items, introduced visible disruptions to reading fluency, thus demanding greater cognitive effort from both children and adults. This contrast suggests that unfamiliar cultural references in translation function as cognitive roadblocks that complicate the negotiation of meaning and significantly alter the reception experience.

Regarding dynamic, audio-visual reading, a new generation of studies has begun transcending the purely linguistic focus of subtitles, shifting towards a more holistic, multimodal approach. Audio-visual reception studies anchored in eye-tracking methodologies have gravitated towards three dominant concerns: how text is processed in real time, how viewers distribute attention across competing visual inputs (image, sound, and speed), and how cognitive effort is modulated by external factors (e.g. d'Ydewalle & De Bruycker, 2007; Szarkowska et al., 2024). Research has increasingly highlighted the intricate cognitive balancing act performed by viewers, in which language proficiency, line segmentation, shot transitions, and translation strategies become pivotal forces shaping the reception process (Perego et al., 2010; Rajendran et al., 2013). Recent investigations, such as that of Kruger, Wisniewska, and Liao (2022), look well beyond textual subtleties, incorporating audio-visual variables such as subtitle speed, dynamic visual environments, and multimodal inputs. These efforts offer a necessary expansion given the fluidity and complexity of multilingual digital content.

Despite its methodological sophistication, eye-tracking research in translation remains constrained by inherent limitations, not least among them small sample sizes and the underrepresentation of key viewer demographics. Furthermore, the cognitive mechanisms of elderly audiences, young viewers, and second-language learners remain underexplored, posing challenges to the generalisability of findings. More broadly, while AVT research using psycholinguistic techniques has matured into a well-established empirical field, its methodological framework faces considerable hurdles when extended to other translation modalities, such as interpreting and localisation. In many ways, our grasp of how static texts are cognitively processed is far more advanced than our understanding of how audiences engage with multimodal, dynamic texts, a discrepancy that underlines the complexities of tracking cognition in participatory and interactive environments.

Technological advancements have undoubtedly broadened our ability to examine cognitive processes in reading, with pupillometry, electroencephalography (EEG), event-related potentials (ERPs), and functional magnetic resonance imaging (fMRI) offering complementary insights into reader cognition. Admittedly, because there have been few empirical attempts (J.-L. Kruger et al., 2017) in this regard, substantial untapped potential remains for refining these cognitive methodologies and developing robust, reliable measures that can translate reading statistics into empirically testable data for dynamic text reception.

Nevertheless, even within these constraints, eye movement and other psychometric measures offer a generative foundation for hypothesis building. Triangulation with offline and qualitative reception data of processing and reception capture interpretive nuances beyond the purely physiological, thereby enriching experimental findings and pushing the field towards a more holistic validation framework (Kruger & Doherty, 2018; Valdez et al., 2025).

3.3 Big Data Analytics and Visualisation

Big data analytics through text-mining techniques, such as collocational networks, keyword extraction, social network mapping, and sentiment analysis, has redefined how we trace the afterlives of translations in digital spaces, making visible the shifting currents of reception across online reading communities and social media (Kotze et al., 2021). Prompted by computational and corpus-linguistic methods, researchers can now listen in on the murmur of collective engagement, capturing readers' perceptions, evaluations, and affective responses in ways that are more reflective of people's reading experiences in naturalistic settings.

With the aforementioned shift comes an interesting paradox. Compared with traditional controlled experiments or carefully designed surveys, big data analytics moves beyond de-contextualised snippets of text and captures reading experiences as naturally embedded; big data-based linguistic evidence is considered unfiltered, unprompted, and generated by real-world interactions (Kotze et al., 2021). In this way, such an approach represents a 'scaling up' of research on reader responses (Kotze et al., 2021: 153). At the same time, the rise of digital reading ecologies has created a kind of panopticon effect in which readers, once engaging freely with online texts, may find themselves unwittingly observed and analysed.

Digital reading communities and social networking platforms, such as Goodreads and Amazon reviews, have transformed the landscape of (translation) reception, aggregating perceptions, and turning the once-private act of reading into public, traceable conversations. These platforms thrive on interactivity, informality, and ephemerality, creating spaces in which reader opinions emerge organically, generated by dialogue and sometimes fleeting impulses. Among these, Goodreads reviews have emerged as an unexpected and powerful big data archive, offering a window into readers' backgrounds and motivations as well as the ripple effects of books in social reading networks (see Hajibayova, 2019; Thelwall, 2019; Walsh & Antoniak, 2021). This extends to translation, particularly of literary works, in which digital communities highlight how readers notice, evaluate, and emotionally engage with texts (see Wang & Humblé, 2020).

A notable case is Kotze et al. (2021), who built the Digital Opinions on Translated Literature (DIOPTRA-L) corpus, a multilingual collection of Goodreads reviews of contemporary literary translations. Their study focused on the salience of translation, specifically on how translations interrupt, surprise, or linger in their experience of the text. Through patterns of emotion and evaluation, they investigated how readers made sense of the concept of translation, sometimes as an invisible presence, other times as a site of friction, curiosity, or even resistance. Crucially, this approach shifts the focus from traditional quality-based translation assessment, which often fixates on linguistic accuracy or fidelity, to the societal expectations, assumptions, and ideologies that influence how readers encounter translations in their own cultural contexts.

What sets this study apart innovatively is its fusion of computational methods and human interpretation to analyse the emotional and evaluative dimensions of translation. Using corpus techniques, such as collocational network analysis and keyword extraction, along with a computational sentiment analysis model, the researchers traced the web of feelings, judgements, and uncertainties surrounding it. By tallying sentiment-laden terms in multilingual texts, the study examined whether certain emotions consistently surfaced in specific genres or translation directions, revealing patterns otherwise buried within vast datasets. More than just a technical feat, this study also demonstrated how big data and computational triangulation could shed light on the cognitive and emotional frameworks that influence reader reception. What emerges is a portrait of reading that is personal and undeniably social.

Unlike traditional researcher-elicited feedback, digital platforms provide organically generated responses, thus allowing researchers to observe reception in its natural habitat rather than through pre-structured questions. Building on actual readers' reactions in social media, Chen (2024) used Rongrong Ren's Chinese translation of *Charlotte's Web* as a case study and examined the paratextual shifts across multiple editions of a translation, exploring how spatial, temporal, substantive, pragmatic, and functional factors interact to influence reception. Using a blend of computational and manual analyses, Chen gathered short comments and long-form reviews from Douban and Shuhua websites, after which the collected online data were filtered and structured using Python-assisted processing.

This approach is consistent with what Gile (1998: 74) called 'non-interactive observational research', a methodological shift that sidesteps the artificiality of retrospective surveys or controlled experiments. A key advantage of this digital landscape is its ability to capture real-time, moment-to-moment shifts in perception. Observing how users' reactions evolve as they engage with translations in fluid everyday settings has long been considered a challenging task. Traditional surveys, although valuable, often fail to account for the subtle recalibrations that occur during the act of reception. At the same time, this paradigm shift challenges the old gatekeeping structures that once made professional readers the dominant arbiters of translation quality. Furthermore, big data analytics for users' immediate reactions to specific translator or interpreter decisions offers a perspective that moves beyond static linguistic judgements towards a more open-ended, experience-driven understanding of reception.

Another virtue of studying online translation reception lies in the ecological perspective it affords. Some video platforms (e.g. BiliBili), with their distinctive *danmu* interface, create compelling spaces for studying audience reception in real time (Yang, 2023). What sets BiliBili's *danmu* apart from conventional comment sections on other platforms (e.g. YouTube) is that, far from being a mere spectacle of digital noise, *danmu* fosters a unique form of participatory voyeurism. This new form allows audiences to react instantly, thereby shaping a collective, evolving interpretation of the content being presented on screen. While YouTube relegates user engagement to a separate space below or beside the video, BiliBili integrates audience responses directly into the content itself, thus serving as a community tool, not mere titillation. As comments flood in at key moments, they generate a 'bullet curtain' effect (Yang, 2020) or a visual manifestation of collective attention and emotional intensity. The denser the comments, the more charged the moment, serving as an indicator of audience engagement that is both qualitative and quantifiable.

Moreover, *danmu*'s significance extends beyond its immediacy. Its timestamped synchronisation ensures that every comment reappears at the exact moment in subsequent viewing sessions, creating an asynchronous and interactive form of discourse. Therefore, users watching days, weeks, or even months later will still experience past audiences' reactions in real time, as if they were engaged in ongoing conversations across time. This synthesis between immediacy and continuity makes *danmu* a fertile site for reception studies in which translating and interpreting are no longer solitary acts of consumption, but social experiences that are particularly shaped and reshaped by a multitude of voices.

However, while computational analysis offers a powerful view of the matrices of translation reception, it does not yield direct answers, but rather opens a field of interpretation with inherent limitations. As stated by Kotze et al. (2021), the collocational network for 'translate' in English-language reviews highlights loose associations rather than firm conclusions, thus demanding further contextualisation. The patterns that emerge in big data remain fragments awaiting synthesis. As such, algorithmic outputs run the risk of being misconstrued as definitive meaning rather than tools for uncovering it, not to mention that the algorithms themselves are not immune to bias. It is even possible that biased algorithms can perpetuate existing inequalities, skewing results in ways that reinforce stereotypes or marginalise certain perspectives. The danger lies in treating these data-driven results as conclusive interpretations when, in reality, they are merely stepping stones in a broader process of analysis and understanding.

Another consideration is the profile of online readers who engage in translation discourse. Although Web 2.0 has democratised user engagement, thus allowing everyday readers to voice their opinions on platforms such as Amazon, Goodreads, and fan forums, this ecosystem is far from universal. The illusion of accessibility belies the asymmetries in participation, especially given that those who post reviews and commentaries represent only a small vocal fraction of the readership. In comparison, many others remain silent. Access to platforms is neither equal nor unmediated; instead, it is conditioned by digital infrastructures and invisible hierarchies of influence. For example, Chen (2023) examined social networking sites and fan forums using data from users who actively discussed translation quality. However, as the study itself acknowledges, digital circulation is unpredictable: Texts may go viral, pirated copies may proliferate across platforms, and audiences may engage in ways that elude capture. Thus, the vast dispersal and volume of online reception data create an analytical paradox: Although there are more data than ever before, truly comprehensive and systematic analyses remain exceedingly difficult.

This sampling bias is particularly evident in reception studies that rely on social media or on-screen comments. The utopian vision of digital participation, once hyped as 'techno-utopianism' (Seymour, 2019: 20), has since been tempered by the realities of algorithmic control. Hu's (2023a) study examines the profound influence of algorithms and media technologies, particularly through streaming giants such as Netflix, on the reception of multilingual films. In this digital age, translator interventions (be it omissions, additions, or explicitations) become powerful tools in sculpting cultural dialogues. These subtitling choices, entwined with Netflix's media logic, fundamentally guide the viewer's understanding, either heightening cultural tensions or nurturing empathy. Thus, rather than fostering genuine plurality, algorithm-driven cultural products tend towards commodification and homogenisation in a world where platform protocols anticipate and mould user behaviours. By contrast, the passive majority, those who consume content without commenting, remain invisible, sidelined, and absent from analyses.

What is noteworthy here is that technologies are never socially or politically neutral in their effects. Digital discourse does not always nurture open debate; rather than being generative, disagreement is often resolved through ritualised humiliation and the 'stiletto-stab' of sadism (Seymour, 2019: 147). As Seymour (2019) warned, social media has trained users to become conduits of informational power, positioning them into both manipulators and the manipulated.

In addition, the strict anonymity of online comments presents another challenge, limiting the possibility of conducting follow-up retrospective studies. Some researchers have suggested embedding *danmu*-based research within controlled conditions, such as curating specific interpreter-mediated events and uploading them to platforms such as BiliBili, thus allowing for targeted participant engagement (Chen et al., 2017). However, although this approach could offer a more structured framework, it risks losing the organic, unscripted nature of digital reception, which makes such studies valuable in the first place.

As John Naughton (2004) observed, when confronted with world-altering technologies, we tend to overestimate their short-term effects and underestimate their long-term consequences. Algorithm-driven translation reception is, at its core, a commodified experience, a process in which, given sufficient data, even the embedded, unconscious axioms shaping behaviour become legible, predictable, and eventually marketable. In this sense, (big data) reception is no longer only about meta-interpretation, but about the forces that condition and constrain what kinds of interpretation are possible.

4 Conditioning Factors Underlying Translation Reception

This section examines the contextual factors that interact to influence the reception of a translation, particularly in high-stakes contexts, when trust (or its erosion) becomes a decisive criterion. It considers the constellation of variables that influence how a translation is perceived: the mode of communication, the linguistic representation of the text, the sociological profile of its audience, the historical and contextual frame in which it emerges, and the ideological positioning of the agent that mediates its interpretation, from the influences of cultural identity to the overt assertions of hierarchical political power. It also questions the complexities of multimodal translation, coupled with technical constraints such as configurations and modalities, which not only convey meaning but also condition perception itself. Beneath these structural considerations lies the fundamental issue of trust, the essential contract between translator and audience that enables the very possibility of communicative success.

4.1 From Linguistic Comprehension to Cognitive Negotiation

The linguistic quality of a translation is often the first battleground in its reception when accuracy and fluency determine not just comprehension but also the reader's trust. A translation that falters, clumsy in its phrasing, awkward in its rhythm, can stir frustration, even suspicion, casting doubt on the translator's competence and intentions.

Language proficiency has long been a common bone of contention. The assumption that linguistic clarity enhances understanding may seem intuitive, but its effects are far from uniform. In her comparative study of two Finnish translations of *The Wizard of Oz*, Puurtinen (1994) found that simplified, reader-friendly linguistic features improved comprehension for younger audiences. However, for adult readers, these modifications had little impact on understanding, while their stylistic preferences varied significantly. Beyond fluency, stylistic perception plays an equally key role in how translations are received. Zasyekin (2010), analysing responses from English and Ukrainian readers, found that translation could produce not just linguistic shifts but also semantic divergences, particularly in literary prose and poetry. Meaning is reshaped and filtered through the structures of language systems. Thus, readability does not equate to acceptability, and translation reception resists easy categorisation.

Cultural allusions further complicate this story. Kenesei (2010), focusing on English–Hungarian poetry translation, similarly found that readers construct meaning through cognitive schemas that differ between source and target texts. The act of translation reception, then, is a reconfiguration of how texts live and resonate within different cultural imaginaries. Leppihalme (1997) examined Finnish readers' responses to foreignisation and literal translation strategies. Her findings suggest that translation acceptance is as much about navigating cultural proximity as it is about linguistic fidelity. Alfvén (2020) investigated the tumultuous translation and reception of two Swedish young-adult novels – *Spelar död* [Play Dead] and *När tågen går förbi* [When the Trains Pass By] – that debuted in France during the 2000s. These works, imbued with unprovoked violence in a realistic style rarely dared by French authors for adolescent audiences, set off a veritable moral maelstrom, igniting fierce debates on the French literary scene. Tracing the stormy reception of these novels, the study uncovered how the chasm between a liberal Swedish source culture and a more conservative French target culture imposes profound constraints on translation reception.

However, readers are not always passive recipients of translation; they can be critical and strategic agents attuned to language distinctness and the word choices that conjure a text's voice. Chen (2022b) found that online readers prioritise linguistic features, such as diction, tone, and rhythm, reflecting a discerning and strategic approach to evaluation. This echoes the 'traditional error-identification linguistic approach' (Chan, 2010: 164) favoured by scholar-critics, in which linguistic precision is scrutinised as a marker of authenticity. Notably, Chen's study found that many readers preferred a source-oriented approach over a target-oriented one, reinforcing the ongoing tension between fidelity and fluency and between remaining true to the original and making a text legible in its new linguistic home.

Nevertheless, reception is not merely a linguistic experience but also cognitively negotiated. The ways in which readers and viewers process translation are mediated, contingent on context, genre, and sensory input. Moran's (2012) eye-tracking study, for example, which explored how word frequency and lexical cohesion influence cognitive effort in subtitle processing, found that less frequent words and lower cohesion significantly increased cognitive load. Concurrently, Perego et al. (2010), in their study of subtitle segmentation, noted that while subtitles do not hinder the processing of accompanying visuals, poorly segmented subtitles result in longer fixation duration, subtly altering cognitive efficiency. That is, the dynamic textual features of subtitles may actively modulate the efficiency of cognitive processing.

This pulsating complexity deepens when multimodal factors come into play in reception. J.-L. Kruger et al. (2022) observed that as subtitle speed escalated, more words were skipped, fewer words were revisited, and complete readings of subtitles became less frequent. These findings suggest that excessive speed limits the time available to resolve ambiguity, ultimately increasing the cognitive burden on viewers. Visual context has emerged as a crucial factor in comprehension. Szarkowska et al. (2024) found that when subtitles were presented without corresponding video, comprehension suffered across all speeds, highlighting the vital role of visual information in reinforcing understanding. This finding challenges traditional interpretations of cognitive load theory, particularly the redundancy principle (Diao & Sweller, 2007), which posits that dual inputs (video and subtitles) may interfere with comprehension. Instead, Szarkowska et al. argued that video is not simply redundant in relation to subtitles but complementary, offering distinct and interconnected ways of sense-making. Unlike the direct overlap between spoken dialogue and subtitles, visual scenes provide additional contextual clues, enriching narrative comprehension rather than competing with textual input. Their findings further suggest that viewers accustomed to subtitles, particularly in cultures in which subtitled media are prevalent, may develop an enhanced ability to integrate multimodal information, allowing them to process multiple and complex audio-visual stimuli with greater ease.

At first glance, quality criteria, such as linguistic and textual dependency, appear to offer a straightforward measure of translation reception. However, this assertion is not without controversy, particularly when set against the illusion of an ideal, catch-all translation. When scholars debate the relative acceptance of domestication versus foreignisation, they risk imposing a reductive, even elitist, binary that frames translation as a site of perpetual antagonism. In practice, however, such rigid divisions rarely hold. Few translations that lean towards foreignisation are entirely devoid of domesticating tendencies, just as those inclined towards domestication inevitably retain echoes of the foreign. More importantly, reception can unfold along a spectrum of openness to the foreign within a text, particularly when readers recognise the foreignness as possessing pedagogical virtue or aesthetic value (Hu, 2022). Some of the most thought-provoking reception ideas operate beyond this false dichotomy, entering into the ever-changing and always incomplete spaces between.

Recent research on subtitling has problematised and challenged the simplistic binary notion of reception, revealing far more flexible and diverse viewer responses. Although one might assume that modifications to subtitle presentation (e.g. increased speed or the removal of audio) would significantly disrupt comprehension, empirical findings tell a different story. Across multiple studies, variables such as faster subtitle speeds (J.-L. Kruger et al., 2022; Szarkowska & Gerber-Morón, 2018) and the absence of sound (Liao et al., 2021; Liao et al., 2022) have been scrutinised, with results revealing that cognitive strain does not always equate to diminished understanding. For example, while higher subtitle speeds do demand greater cognitive effort, they primarily alter reading patterns rather than outright comprehension. Eye-tracking data suggest that increased speeds lead to shorter and fewer fixations, longer saccades, and reduced crossovers between subtitles and images, resulting in more surface-level processing.

Curiously, comprehension appears more resilient than one might expect. Liao et al. (2022) examined how auditory and visual stimuli interact with subtitle reading among native Chinese speakers of English as a second language. Their findings demonstrate that the presence of audio, whether in the source or in the target language, reduced reliance on subtitles in distinct ways: Chinese audio led to more superficial processing, while English audio encouraged better engagement, pointing to the role of metacognitive strategies in multilingual comprehension. Here, reception is about weighting multiple streams of information and constantly trying to look for a point of balance between linguistic familiarity and cognitive effort.

In an effort to account for these cognitive mechanisms, Kruger and Liao (2022) submitted a multimodal integrated-language model, drawing on Reichle's (2021) computational model of reading. According to their model, viewers can track a limited set of familiar visual elements while simultaneously processing subtitles during an initial pre-attentive visual phase. Once identified, these factors become linked to propositional content in working memory, contributing to the formation of an evolving situation. By accommodating the serial allocation of attention, this framework explains how viewers can move between visual monitoring and reading, preserving comprehension even at higher subtitle speeds.

Taken together, these studies complicate the notion that reception is purely linguistic or that cognitive effort alone determines comprehension. Instead, understanding takes shape through a finely balanced negotiation of text, image, and sound, serving as an active, adaptive process through which the mind orchestrates disparate inputs into a whole.

4.2 Culture Distances, Emotions, and Affective Translation

Cultural distance operates as another fundamental premise in the reception of translation. The extent to which a translation is accepted hinges on how cultural allusions and culture-bound references are reconciled. Leppihalme's (1997) pioneering study exposed Finnish readers to translated excerpts from journalistic and fictional texts embedded with cultural references. Through open-ended responses, she uncovered a recurring tension: When cultural allusions are rendered too literally, they risk patronising or even alienating readers, generating cognitive friction rather than fostering understanding. In much the same vein, Liang's (2007) study on *Harry Potter* translations in Taiwan found that children responded more favourably to localised cultural elements than to those that remained anchored in the source culture, highlighting the role of familiarity in reception. As Kotze et al. (2021) suggested, translation directionality does not function as a rigid determinant of reception; rather, its influence is mediated by genre and the interpretive habits that affect how readers engage with foreignness.

Reader reception is moulded by the confluence of cultural familiarity, perceptual differences, and linguistic expertise. Each reader's unique cognitive makeup and naturalistic profiles finely construe the interpretation. As H. Kruger (2012) demonstrated through eye-tracking data, the paths taken by adults and children diverge markedly when they process cultural items in translation. Adult readers, enriched by broader meta-awareness, can align new information with real-world experiences and genre expectations. This capacity allows them to pause and ponder culturally unfamiliar or unexpected elements, albeit without necessarily derailing their overall grasp of the text. By contrast, young readers tend to sift through the written word, applying a more immediate, almost instinctive process guided by word frequency and the clarity of grapheme-to-phoneme mapping. For them, meaning is often distilled from basic textual cues, and unfamiliar cultural references tend to slip by unnoticed unless they present a stark interruption. When such disruptions do occur, they demand considerable cognitive effort, frequently leading to a more pronounced decline in comprehension than has been observed among adults.

Such a cognitive differential is intertwined with readers' idiosyncratic identities. Likewise, the perceived quality of an interpretation emerges from sociocultural dynamics that extend beyond mere linguistic mechanics. Attributes such as the interpreter's persona (Cheung, 2020), the degree of listener reliance on interpretation (Setton & Dawrant, 2016), and the relationship between this dependence and quality judgements (Cheung, 2022) all contribute to its evaluation. The rejection of an accent, for example, may serve as a surrogate for a broader repudiation of the cultural symbols it embodies (Lippi-Green, 1997). Cheung (2013) further noted that some participants expressed a preference for the English source language over the accented simultaneous renderings, hinting at long-running sociocultural undercurrents. Furthermore, Cheung (2022) posited that the state–society dynamics between mainland China and Hong Kong profoundly affect local perceptions of interpreters with a mainland accent. During the heightened political tensions of early 2020, this social tension seemingly intensified negative attitudes towards Mandarin, as reflected in a markedly greater reliance on Cantonese renderings for Mandarin content, forming an expression, albeit implicit, of a desire to assert a distinct social identity.

In this light, the social value that readers attribute to a translation becomes interesting and important on several grounds. Wardle (2019: 235) contended that while some readers select a translation based on its inherent quality, many are swayed by external influences, such as availability, marketing strategies, and peer reviews. Karas (2020) examined the role of intelligibility in intralingual translations, indicating how reader comprehension influences perceptions of a translation's necessity and legitimacy. By examining the Modern Hebrew translation of the Hebrew Bible, Karas illustrates that intelligibility, traditionally associated with spoken language, extends to the written word, thereby influencing judgements about a translation's value and its educational and cultural implications.

Rather than existing as a homogeneous mass, readers are positioned along gradients of influence and authority, a stratification that profoundly affects the acceptance of translations. This hierarchical structure complicates the immediate reception and the ever-evolving, long-term social implications of translated texts. As Fish (1980: 223) demonstrated, power dynamics within reader communities can shift as groups interact, with the voices of opinion leaders exerting a disproportionate impact on collective judgement. In this way, the stratified nature of readership, embedded in and constrained by social relations, further essentialises our understanding of translation acceptance.

4.3 Trust Thrives in Translation Reception

What remains intriguing is the extent to which readers trust the translator's varied interventions. This trust, tempered by each reader's assurance of the mediators and their acquaintance with the source culture, profoundly affects expectations and interpretations. The intricacies of trust have been examined across disciplines, from behaviourist psychology to systems sociology, and they are widely acknowledged as indispensable to translation as effective communication. As Chesterman (2016) astutely observed, without trust, the very edifice of the translation profession (and its praxis) would inevitably crumble.

One may suggest that trust imbues translation reception with a profound ethical vector. Readers begin in a somewhat suspicious frame of mind, and their faith in the text can be irrevocably undermined through various channels. One key issue lies in the perception of translation as inherently inferior to the original, a notion frequently intertwined with doubts about the translator's credibility. In examining the online reception of literary works, Kotze et al. (2021) found that, although translation itself may not be at the forefront of a reader's mind, it becomes a focal point in the wake of poor reviews. When misunderstandings arise, sceptical readers intuitively suspect the translation and instinctively assign blame to the translator, considering translation a convenient scapegoat for their dissatisfaction. This phenomenon reflects a broader mistrust of translators and an enduring belief in the primacy of the source text, which can ultimately colour the reading experience with an air of deficiency. Similarly, Wardle's (2012) examination of an Italian translation of *Alice's Adventures in Wonderland* deftly illustrates how the translator's reputation, which serves as an implicit paratext, can decisively influence public trust, thereby shaping the reception of both the translation and its original counterpart.

Misunderstandings can breed distrust to the point that communication is severely curtailed. In their study on the reception of machine-translated subtitles, Qiu and Pym (2024) found that errors surpassing an acceptable threshold eroded viewers' trust. This erosion compromised comprehension and, by extension, the viewing experience. The cumulative impact of recurring errors may eventually overwhelm viewers' tolerance, critically undermining the perceived credibility of the translation. At a certain point, this loss of credibility renders the subtitles so untrustworthy that they cease to function as valid translations, risking dismissal, rejection, or even ridicule (Pym, 2015, 2025).

If readers trust that the translator intervention is well intended, they are more likely to accept translations with a higher level of intervention. For instance, empirical research indicates that when reading 'foreignised' texts, if readers believe in the value of the exotic, of the foreign milieu that remains partly mysterious, unknown, and thus awaiting discovery, they may be inclined to invest additional cognitive effort in accepting an obscure text (Hu 2022, 2023b). In this sense, readers are more likely to accept the translation has pedagogical value in enabling them to explore new worlds, albeit with some imperfections. Aesthetic pleasure arises from exploring new points of view and accommodating uncertainties in our understanding (Qiu & Pym, 2024).

Trust serves as a noticeable factor in determining the extent to which readers tolerate deviations from their expectations. Chiaro (2004) explored how varying degrees of trust influence a television audience's acceptance of a host-interpreter's performance, revealing that trust is indispensable for genuine satisfaction and engagement. Edwards et al. (2005) further illustrated this theme through semi-structured interviews with migrant groups and uncovered that trust, forged through previous encounters with public service interpreting, underpins expectations and perceptions of quality. For these participants, 'good interpreting' is defined also by the reliability and integrity of service, a standard built on trust. As reported in Qiu and Pym (2024), in instances in which a viewer's engagement with audio-visual content outweighs the disquiet generated by machine-translated errors, trust becomes the defining nature of the interaction, balancing divergent expectations and fostering a trade-off decision between fidelity and creative expression.

As we noted, readers can never be deemed infallible. Hoff and Bashir's (2014) study suggested that self-confidence plays a key role in shaping trust and guiding decision-making. With the ascendancy of English as a lingua franca, more users feel empowered to assess an interpreter's performance. For example, listeners' perceptions are often tinged with bias, as documented by Cheung (2020), and their reliance on the interpretation collectively informs their ever-shifting evaluations. Another example is Hu's (2022) exploration of Australian responses to varied translations of Chinese political discourse. Some readers favoured a foreignised, literal rendering of the idiom 桃李不言 (*taoli buyan*), translated simply as 'peaches and plums do not speak', but they struggled to capture its full nuance. In the source text, this idiom, which was used by President Xi Jinping, was intended to extol the merits of the China-led Belt and Road initiative. Australian readers, however, engaged in imaginative reinterpretations of the low-intervention translation. One respondent considered the idiom as evoking the allure of a tree offering cool, inviting shade, a kind of *locus amoenus* that beckons fruit pickers. Although this 'shade' metaphor might not be inherent to the original phrase, the presidential use of the idiom recasts the initiative as a protective umbrella for shared interests. Other readers confessed to not fully grasping the idiom's meaning but expressed fondness for its literal translation, remarking that it evoked 'a bit of imagery'. This trust, in turn, fosters a negotiation in which readers balance the immersive pleasure of engagement with their willingness to accept a measure of foreignness.

It is instructive to apply the distinction between 'thick' and 'thin' trust (Hosking, 2014: 46–49; Putnam, 2000; see also Rizzi, Lang, & Pym, 2019; Pym 2025) to translation reception. This dichotomy, emerging from the erosion of social capital in the neoliberal era, captures a shift from a rich, interpersonal engagement (what might be called 'thick trust') to a narrower, more utilitarian form ('thin trust'). In institutional settings, Hu (2020) observed that Chinese government interpreters who nurtured genuine interpersonal rapport with their superiors were more inclined to deviate from rigid literalism, offering translations imbued with creative nuance. Their latitude stemmed from a reservoir of 'thick trust', in which they were recognised as individuals rather than as mere functionaries. One interpreter recalled how a superior, who was an avid reader of *The Wall Street Journal*, accepted the use of English idiomatic expressions in speeches rather than insisting on a strictly literal rendition of Chinese political jargon. In stark contrast, other in-house interpreters treated the original Chinese discourse as sacrosanct, clinging to literalism with a reverence bordering on superstition, wary of subjecting it to any test-by-fire. In contexts in which trust is scant, such rigidity constrains creative problem solving. In the absence of trust, literalism may seem a safe fallback.

Another striking illustration of this dynamic emerges in the context of diplomatic press conferences held by the Chinese government. At first glance, the primary recipients appear to be foreign journalists tasked with disseminating the translated message to a global audience. However, the audience is multifaceted: Chinese spokespersons and diplomats present at the event vigilantly assess whether the communication conforms to established institutional norms, while keen China watchers, such as foreign political analysts, scrutinise every detail of the proceedings. Notably, Chinese institutional interpreters, though ostensibly addressing non-Chinese-speaking journalists, actually prioritise the expectations of Chinese bilingual officials and colleagues who prefer strict literalism. While the overt objective is to serve target language users, the underlying imperative is one of internal censorship and maintaining power structures. For Chinese institutional interpreters, linguistic fidelity is often conflated with ideological allegiance to communism (Hu, 2020). Simultaneously, this approach exposes deep-seated distrust among Chinese bureaucrats and interpreters of foreign interpretations. This is a manifestation of trust as a tool of power control. Although literalism may appear to be a risk-averse strategy, it ultimately stifles the potential for genuine intercultural dialogue. In the absence of trust, interpretations are tightly regulated, and intercultural communication inevitably comes to a standstill.

4.4 Trade-Off Acceptance of Technology Intervention

In multilingual societies, translations generated by translation technology and large language models have become ubiquitous and intertwined with our daily lives. Economic constraints often relegate the production of personalised, universally accessible materials by human translators to the realm of powerful stakeholders and major languages, particularly when viewed through the lens of accessibility. In response to these limitations, many scholars advocate a rigorous evaluation of how technology-generated outputs are received and accepted as a means to enhance linguistic clarity and sensory accessibility.

For example, Hu et al. (2020) examined how Chinese audiences engaged with unrefined MT subtitles for massive open online courses (MOOCs), using Chesterman's (2007) '3 R framework (i.e., reactions, responses, and repercussions)' as a conceptual tool, which is later adapted to audio-visual translation by Gambier (2018). Their study found that, for most Chinese viewers, MT-generated subtitles from English to Chinese held promise for nurturing long-term pedagogical advancement. Likewise, Matamala and Ortiz-Boix (2016) explored the potential of MT for audio descriptions and proposed it as a viable solution to boost accessibility in multilingual contexts. Their study, which examined filmic audio descriptions translated from Catalan into Spanish, relied on text-based error analysis rather than direct user engagement to assess the quality of machine-generated outputs. The authors contend that post-editing machine outputs, as opposed to crafting new audio descriptions for each language from scratch, could streamline processes, optimise resources, and ultimately broaden accessibility.

Conversely, as MT algorithms gain credibility, reception studies also turn their attention to the quality of technology-generated subtitles, scrutinising them through meticulous analyses of translation errors. For example, Romero-Fresco and Pérez (2015) introduced an error typology known as the NER model, in which 'N' denotes the number of words, 'E' the editing errors, and 'R' the recognition of errors, to examine the unsuspected complexities of intralingual live subtitling. Drawing inspiration from this framework, Pedersen's (2017) FAR model offers a more nuanced approach to evaluating interlingual subtitles by examining their functional equivalence 'F', accuracy 'A', and readability 'R'.

Recent scholarly enquiry has increasingly explored the challenges of integrating MT into translation reception, especially in audio-visual contexts. Tuominen et al. (2023) investigated the role of automated subtitling in enhancing the linguistic accessibility of public broadcasts. Through focus groups and questionnaires, they looked into how English-speaking audiences processed Finnish-language news clips with automated subtitles, scrutinising comprehension, acceptability, and self-reported cognitive load. Their findings unveiled an intriguing duality: While viewers generally grasped the overarching narrative, disruptions caused by timing inconsistencies and translation errors imposed significant cognitive strain. Interestingly, the study also highlighted that viewers' motivation and interest profoundly influenced their tolerance of suboptimal subtitles. Those with a strong desire (or necessity) to access audio-visual material demonstrated greater patience with imperfections, suggesting that engagement with automated subtitles is as much a matter of context and intent as it is of quality.

MT has increasingly permeated high-stakes environments, but its reception remains conspicuously uncharted and marked by an imbalance that favours producers over receivers (Nunes Vieira et al., 2023). Nevertheless, another dimension beckons. Traditional evaluation metrics and linguistic taxonomies (Costa et al., 2015; Vilar et al., 2006) have long served as tools for product assessment, but they often neglect the lived experience of reception. In the realm of MT, both automatic and manual methods have focused primarily on semantic precision and grammatical correctness. However, the inherent uncertainty of imperfect machine outputs invites a spectrum of responses, some of which are tinged with pervasive technophobia. At times, readers cast aside translated texts altogether, their scepticism a direct repudiation of machine intervention. More broadly, Sakamoto and Yamada (2020) explore the ongoing negotiations surrounding machine translation post-editing (MTPE), in which various social groups (project managers, clients, and translators) impose their own attitudes onto the practice, conditioned by their roles, desires, and expectations. These differing interpretations show underlying power structures at play: project managers are divided between proponents and sceptics of translation technologies; clients weigh the trade-offs of cost, time, and quality; and translators grapple with their own ambivalence towards engaging in MTPE. The findings suggest that the future of MTPE hinges on a balance of these competing interests, emphasising the need for ethical and sustainable workflows within the ever-evolving translation industry. Here, my enquiry shifts from the mere quality assessment of machine-generated output to a more critical exploration of how readers negotiate the delicate trade-off between errors and efficiency, creating a compromise that reconciles the imperfections of translation with the pragmatic allure of technological advancement.

Effective communication depends on a delicate weighting of reader trust and the acceptance of technological imperfections. Qiu and Pym (2024) looked into how MT errors in subtitles affect viewer trust and engagement. Their findings showed that while a monotonous, bland output could be overlooked, errors that generate significant misunderstanding and erode trust prove 'fatal', shattering immersion and driving audiences away. However, many viewers exhibit notable resilience, filtering out misinformation and seeking alternative cues to construct meaning. Thus, this study highlights the trade-off between technological imperfections and the trust necessary for a satisfying audio-visual experience. Similarly, Pym, Ayvazyan, and Prioleau (2022) remarked that although MT has become indispensable for the cost-effective dissemination of critical health information, its efficacy rests on the fragile bedrock of trust. When audiences deem these algorithmically generated messages reliable (even in their unrefined state), their confidence fuels their action. However, when glaring errors surface, their trust shrinks, thus causing bewilderment, withdrawal, and, eventually, the alienation of those the communication was meant to serve.

This tolerance is contextualised as part of a broader trade-off between the enjoyment of the viewing experience and the variability in viewers' knowledge of the source language. At any rate, an apparently major linguistic omission caused by machine intervention may not confuse viewers if other channels help bridge the information gap. This echoes the cognitive framework proposed by Liao et al. (2022), which suggests that for viewers, visual components can be associated with propositional content held in working memory, derived from subtitles, thus contributing to the formation of an evolving situation model. Nevertheless, misunderstandings can cause a chain effect (Pedersen, 2017) in which serious errors not only affect viewers' comprehension of a subtitle line but also cause problems with framing interpretations of later lines. Distrust in technology-enabled translational communication can accumulate to the point where the target reader simply loses patience and gives up on the translation. After all, translation acceptance may be viewed as a gradation of responses, each marked by varying degrees of trade-offs, rather than a simple yes-or-no verdict.

5 Epilogue

Translation reception is far too broad to be encapsulated by a single name. However, to deny that translation depends on its reception is to retreat into the illusory comfort of isolation. Such an illusion perpetuates the idea that source text and its translation remain untouched by the social currents, cultural collisions, and inevitable contingencies of real life. Instead, reception forms the very machinery of translation, serving as a continuous feedback loop in which all stakeholders, including authors, translators, and readers, invite and absorb it in a most tangible, human sense.

Research on translation reception has flourished in recent years. Current scholarship has seen a quiet and profound emergence of translation reception research long residing at the margins of translation studies but now thriving amidst a wave of interdisciplinarity, advanced cognitive approaches, and big data analytics. In this regard, this Element seeks to harmonise the cognitive and social dimensions of reception across translations in multimodalities, arguing that these epistemological presuppositions need not evolve independently but rather in concert, as demonstrated by conceptual theories and empirical studies that reveal their interconnected nature (cf. Kruger & Kruger 2017).

What sets research on translation reception apart from other target-oriented paradigms or linguistically focused quality assessments is its focus on the sociocognitive implications of the translator's intervention upon actual readers, positioning translation as a form of mediation that may, albeit not always successfully, engender trust and influence the reader's engagement with the text. The ethical imperative for trust building, formed between the translator and the reader, is the cornerstone upon which intercultural communication rests. In this sense, reception studies offer a promising avenue for deepening cultural dialogue and proposing tentative solutions to long-standing conflicts between communities with divergent ideological perspectives.

Moreover, reader expectations can be understood, in the most general sense, as independent repositories of interpretations, each like a Chinese box, harbouring its own sociocultural underpinnings. In some cases, familiarity with the source culture or with the translator's style can mitigate the risks of suspicion, while in others, a preference for a literal rendering may be chosen to avoid potential distortion. Epistemologically, receiving a translation can be construed as an exercise in managing risk. Rational readers invest considerable effort in processing high-stakes texts, weighing linguistic fidelity against ethical considerations and the possibility of manipulation (Pym, 2020, 2025).

What I have aimed to explore and theorise in this Element is to unwrap the core of reception by fleshing out an acknowledgement that reception is inherently contingent, offering no act of closure and continually open for revision, change and thus possibility. The nonlinear trade-off model of reception proposed in this work elucidates how linguistic and ethical factors must be balanced against one another to optimise mutual benefits in intercultural communication, but only if a certain degree of trust is fostered among all stakeholders, thereby tempering the latent risks (Hu, 2023b).

In our current era marked by rapid technological progress and emerging sociocultural realities, one may be tempted to hold techno-utopian visions of information flow. Nevertheless, it is interesting to see that such cyber-idealism can swiftly give way to cyber-cynicism when technology generates not trust but a cascade of errors, misunderstandings, and miscommunications. The future of translation reception may very well lie in navigating trust upon a foundation of ambiguities, uncertainties, and paradoxes, granting us the epistemological and methodological confidence to navigate these challenges.

After all, the success of translation is measured not solely by accuracy or fluency but also by the extent to which it is *trusted* in reception. As we now live in a perpetual state of unpredictability, how can this delicate balance ever be achieved in practice? We shall wait and see.

References

Aleksandrowicz, P. (2020). Can subtitles for the deaf and hard-of-hearing convey the emotions of film music? A reception study. *Perspectives*, 28(1), 58–72.

Alfvén, V. (2020). Defying norms through unprovoked violence: The translation and reception of two Swedish young adult novels in France. In J. Van Coillie and J. McMartin, eds., *Children's Literature in Translation: Texts and Contexts*. Leuven: Leuven University Press, pp. 263–76.

Allington, D. (2007). 'How come most people don't see it?': Slashing the Lord of the Rings. *Social Semiotics*, 17(1), 43–62.

Alvstad, C. (2010). Children's literature and translation. In Y. Gambier and L. van Doorslaer, eds., *Handbook of Translation Studies*, vol. 11. Amsterdam: John Benjamins, pp. 22–7.

Ameri, S. & Khoshsaligheh, M. (2020). An experiment on amateur and professional subtitling reception in Iran. *SKASE Journal of Translation and Interpretation*, 14(2), 2–21.

Andringa, E. (2006). Penetrating the Dutch polysystem: The reception of Virginia Woolf, 1920–2000. *Poetics Today*, 27(3), 501–68.

Angelelli, C. V. (2004). *Revisiting the Interpreter's Role: A Study of Conference, Court, and Medical Interpreters in Canada, Mexico, and the United States*, Amsterdam: John Benjamins.

Angelelli, C. V. (ed.) (2014). *The Sociological Turn in Translation and Interpreting Studies*, Amsterdam: John Benjamins.

Arrojo, R. (1997). Asymmetrical relations of power and the ethics of translation. *TEXTconTEXT*, 11(1), 5–24.

Athique, A. (2016). *Transnational Audiences: Media Reception on a Global Scale*, Cambridge: Polity Press.

Baer, B. J. (2014). Translated literature and the role of the reader. In S. Bermann and C. Porter, eds., *A Companion to Translation Studies*. West Sussex: Wiley, pp. 333–44.

Baker, M. (2006). *Translation and Conflict: A Narrative Account*, London: Routledge.

Batchelor, K. (2018). *Translation and Paratext*, London: Routledge.

Bell, A. (1984). Language style as audience design. *Language in Society*, 13, 145–204.

Berk Albachten, Ö. & Tahir Gürçağlar, Ş. (eds.) (2019). *Perspectives on Retranslation: Ideology, Paratexts, Methods*, New York: Routledge.

Berman, A. (1990). La retraduction comme espace de la traduction [Retranslation as translation space]. *Palimpsestes*, 41, 1–7.

Bhabha, H. (1994). *The Location of Culture*, New York: Routledge.

Bosseaux, C. (2007). *How Does It Feel? Point of View in Translation: The Case of Virginia Woolf into French*, Amsterdam: Rodopi.

Braun, S. (2018). Video-mediated interpreting in legal settings in England. Interpreters' perceptions in their sociopolitical context. *Translation and Interpreting Studies*, 13(3), 393–420.

Brems, E. & Pinto, S. R. (2013). Reception and translation. In Y. Gambier and L. Van Doorslaer, eds., *Handbook of Translation Studies*, vol. 4. Amsterdam: John Benjamins, pp. 142–7.

Briechle, L. & Eppler, E. D. (2019). Swearword strength in subtitled and dubbed films: A reception study. *Intercultural Pragmatics*, 16(4), 389–420. https://doi.org/10.1515/ip-2019-0021.

Bühler, H. (1986). Linguistic (semantic) and extra-linguistic (pragmatic) criteria for the evaluation of conference interpreters and interpretation. *Multilingua*, 5(4), 411–39.

Chan, T. L. (2009). Reading the global: The reader-consumer and the Murakami translation phenomenon in China. *Translation Quarterly*, 53/54, 1–46.

Chan T. H. (2010) *Readers, reading and reception of translated fiction in Chinese: Novel encounters*. Manchester: St. Jerome.

Chang, N. F. (2011). In defence of polysystem theory. *Target*, 23(22), 311–47.

Chatman, S. (1978). *Narrative Structure in Fiction and Film*, Ithaca, NY: Cornell University Press.

Chen, X. (2022a). Retranslation as an intertextual space: Textual and paratextual analysis of two Chinese translations of E. B. White's The Trumpet of the Swan. *Translation Studies*, 15(2), 173–87.

Chen, X. (2022b). Interactive reception of online literary translation: The translator-readers dynamics in a discussion forum. *Perspectives*, 31(4), 690–704.

Chen, X. (2023). The role of childhood nostalgia in the reception of translated children's literature. *Target*, 35(4), 595–620.

Chen, X. (2024). The role of spatial changes to paratext in literary translation reception: Eleven Chinese editions of Charlotte's Web. *Translation Studies*, 17(2), 299–313.

Chen, Y. M. (2011). The translator's subjectivity and its constraints in news transediting: A perspective of reception aesthetics. *Meta*, 56(1), 119–44.

Chen, Y., Gao, Q. & Patrick Rau, P.-L. (2017). Watching a movie alone yet together: Understanding reasons for watching Danmaku videos. *International Journal of Human-Computer Interaction*, 33(9), 731–43.

Chesterman, A. (2007). Bridge concepts in translation sociology. In M. Wolf and A. Fukari, eds., *Constructing a Sociology of Translation*. Amsterdam: John Benjamins, pp. 171–83.

Chesterman, A. (1998). Causes, translations, effects. *Target*, 10(2), 201–30.

Chesterman, A. (1993). From 'is' to 'ought'. Laws, norms and strategies in translation studies. *Target*, 1(5), 1–20.

Chesterman, A. (2016). *Memes of Translation: The Spread of Ideas in Translation Theory*, revised ed., Amsterdam: John Benjamins.

Cheung, A. K. F. (2020). Interpreters' perceived characteristics and perception of quality in interpreting. *Interpreting*, 22(1), 35–55.

Cheung, A. K. F. (2022). Listeners' perception of the quality of simultaneous interpreting and perceived dependence on simultaneous interpreting. *Interpreting*, 24(1), 38–58.

Cheung, A. K. F. (2013). Non-native accents and simultaneous interpreting quality perceptions. *Interpreting*, 15(1), 25–47.

Chiaro, D. (2004). Investigating the perception of translated verbally expressed humour on Italian TV. *ESP across Cultures*, 1(1), 35–52.

Christensen, T. P. (2011). User expectations and evaluation: A case study of a court interpreting event. *Studies in Translation Theory and Practice*, 19(1), 1–24.

Cohen A. J., MacMillan K. & Drew R. (2006). The role of music, sound effects & speech on absorption in a film: The congruence-associationist model of media cognition. *Canadian Acoustics*, 34(3), 40–41.

Collados Aís, Á., Pradas Macías, E. M., Stévaux, E. & García Becerra, O. (eds.) (2007). *La Evaluación de la Calidad en Interpretación Simultánea: Parámetros de Incidencia* [Quality Assessment in Simultaneous Interpretation: Incidence Parameters], Granada: Comares.

Collados Aís, Á. (2002). Quality assessment in simultaneous interpreting: The importance of nonverbal communication. In F. Pöchhacker and M. Shlesinger, eds., T*he Interpreting Studies Reader*. London: Routledge, pp. 327–36.

Costa, Â., Ling, W., Luís, T., Correia, R. & Coheur, L. (2015). A linguistically motivated taxonomy for machine translation error analysis. *Machine Translation*, 29(2), 127–61.

Cross, G. (2018). Historical roots of consumption-based nostalgia for childhood in the United States. In E. Wesseling, ed., *Reinventing Childhood Nostalgia: Books, Toys, and Contemporary Media Culture*. London: Routledge, pp. 19–35.

Davies, W. (2015). *The Happiness Industry: How the Government and Big Business Sold Us Well-Being*. London: Verso.

Deane-Cox, S. (2014). *Retranslation: Translation, Literature and Reinterpretation*, London: Bloomsbury.

De Boe, E. (2023). *Remote Interpreting in Healthcare Settings*, Berlin: Peter Lang.

Demirkol Ertürk, Ş. (2023). Remembered in translation: Retranslators of William Saroyan into Turkish as guardians of erased memories. *The Translator*, 30(2), 227–48.

Diao, Y. & Sweller, J. (2007). Redundancy in foreign language reading comprehension instruction: Concurrent written and spoken presentations. *Learning and Instruction*, 17(1), 78–88.

Díaz Cintas, J. & Szarkowska, A. (2020). Introduction: Experimental research in audiovisual translation – Cognition, reception, production. *The Journal of Specialised Translation*, 33, 3–16.

Di Giovanni, E. (2018). Dubbing, perception and reception. In E. Di Giovanni and Y. Gambier, eds., *Reception Studies and Audiovisual Translation*. Amsterdam: John Benjamins, pp. 159–77.

Di Giovanni, E. & Gambier, Y. (eds.) (2018). *Reception Studies and Audiovisual Translation*, Amsterdam: John Benjamins.

Downie, J. (2024). A critical review of church interpreting research. *Interpreting and Society*, 4(1), 67–94.

D'Ydewalle, G. & De Bruycker, W. (2007). Eye movements of children and adults while reading television subtitles. *European Psychologist*, 12(3), 196–205.

Edwards, R., Temple, B. & Alexander, C. (2005). Users' experiences of interpreters: The critical role of trust. *Interpreting*, 7(1), 77–95.

Eker Roditakis, A. (2017). Reviewers as readers with power: What a case of retranslation says about author, translator and reader dynamics. *Mémoires du livre/Studies in Book Culture*, 9(1), 1–30.

Escudero, T. (2022). Metatranslational discourse in poetry translators' prefaces. *The Translator*, 28(3), 279–94.

Even-Zohar, I. (1978). The position of translated literature within the literary polysystem. In J. S. Holmes, J. Lambert and R. van den Broeck, eds., *Literature and Translation*. Leuven: Acco, pp. 117–27.

Fillmore, C. (1977). Scenes-and-frames semantics. In A. Zambolli, ed., *Linguistic Structure Processing*. Amsterdam: North Holland, pp. 55–82.

Fish, S. (1980). *Is There a Text in This Class? The Authority of Interpretive Communities*, Cambridge, MA: Harvard University Press.

Gadamer, H. G. (1975). Truth and method. *Journal of Aesthetics and Art Criticism*, 36(4), 487–90.

Gambier, Y. (2018). Translation studies, audiovisual translation and reception. In E. Di Giovanni and Y. Gambier, eds., *Reception Studies and Audiovisual Translation*. Amsterdam: John Benjamins, pp. 43–66.

Garzone, G. (2002). Quality and norms in interpretation. In G. Garzone and M. Viezzi, eds., *Interpreting in the 21st century: Challenges and Opportunities*. Amsterdam: John Benjamins, pp. 107–19.

Genette, G. (1997). *Paratexts: Thresholds of Interpretation*, J. E. Lewin, trans., New York: Cambridge University Press.

Gile, D. (1998). Observational studies and experimental studies in the investigation of conference interpreting. *Target*, 10(1), 69–93.

Goldhill, S. (2002). *Who Needs Greek? Contests in the Cultural History of Hellenism*, New York: Cambridge University Press.

Grbić, N. (2008). Constructing interpreting quality. *Interpreting*, 10(2), 232–57.

Greco, G. M. (2018). The nature of accessibility studies. *Journal of Audiovisual Translation*, 1(1), 205–32.

Hajibayova, L. (2019). Investigation of Goodreads' reviews: Kakutanied, deceived or simply honest? *Journal of Documentation*, 75(3), 612–26.

Hale, S. B. (2004). *The Discourse of Court Interpreting: Discourse Practices of the Law, the Witness and the Interpreter*, Amsterdam: John Benjamins.

Hale, S. B. (2006). Themes and methodological issues in court interpreting research. In E. Hertog and B. van der Veer, eds., *Taking Stock: Research and Methodology in Community Interpreting*. Antwerp: Hoger Instituut voor Vertalers & Tolken, pp. 205–28.

Hale, S. (2007). *Community Interpreting*. Basingstoke: Palgrave Macmillan.

Halverson, S. & Kotze, H. (2022). Sociocognitive constructs in translation and interpreting studies (TIS). Do we really need concepts like norms and risk when we have a comprehensive usage-based theory of language? In S. L. Halverson and Á. Marín García, eds., *Contesting Epistemologies in Cognitive Translation and Interpreting Studies*. London: Routledge, pp. 51–79.

Hoff, K. A. & Bashir, M. (2014). Trust in automation: Integrating empirical evidence on factors that influence trust. *Human Factors*, 57(3), 407–34.

Horton, D. & Wohl, R. (1956). Mass communication and para-social interaction observations on intimacy at a distance. *Psychiatry*, 19(3), 215–29.

Hosking, G. (2014). *Trust: A History*, Oxford: Oxford University Press.

Hu, B. (2020). How are translation norms negotiated? A case study of risk management in Chinese institutional translation. *Target*, 32(1), 83–121.

Hu, B. (2022). Feeling foreign: A trust-based compromise model of translation reception. *Translation Studies*, 15(2), 202–20.

Hu, B. (2023a). Translating intercultural interactions in the Netflix-branded film *American Factory*. *Target*, 35(3), 378–403.

Hu, B. (2023b). Flowing to the reception side. A trade-off model of translation acceptance. In I. Feinauer, A. Marais and M. Swart, eds., *Translation Flows: Exploring Networks of People, Processes and Products*. Amsterdam: John Benjamins, pp. 183–206.

Işıklar Koçak, M. & Erkul Yağcı, A. S. (2019). Readers and retranslation: Transformation in readers' habituses in Turkey from the 1930s to the 2010s. In Ö. Berk Albachten and Ş. Tahir Gürçağlar, eds., *Perspectives on Retranslation: Ideology, Paratexts, Methods*. New York: Routledge, pp. 129–47.

Jakobsen, A. L. (2017). Translation process research. In J. W. Schwieter and A. Ferreira, eds., *The Handbook of Translation and Cognition*. Hoboken, NJ: Wiley-Blackwell, pp. 21–49.

Jakobsen, A. L. & Alves, F. (2020). Introduction. In F. Alves and A. L. Jakobsen, eds., *The Routledge Handbook of Translation and Cognition*. Abingdon: Routledge, pp. 1–22.

Jauss, H. R. (1982). *Toward an Aesthetic of Reception*, Minneapolis, MN: University of Minnesota Press.

Jiménez-Crespo, M. A. (2011). From many one: Novel approaches to translation quality in a social network era. *Linguistica Antverpiensia, New Series–Themes in Translation Studies*, 10, 131–52.

Just, M. A. & Carpenter, P. A. (1980). A theory of reading: From eye fixations to comprehension. *Psychological Review*, 87(4), 329–54.

Kaczmarek, L. (2016). Towards a broader approach to the community interpreter's role: On correspondence between role perceptions and interactional goals. *Interpreting*, 18(1), 57–88.

Kalina, S. (2004). Zum Qualitätsbegriff beim Dolmetschen [Quality in interpreting]. *Lebende Sprachen*, 1, 2–8.

Karas, H. (2020). Intelligibility and the reception of translations. *Perspectives*, 28(1), 24–42.

Kelly, A. M. (2000). Cultural parameters for interpreters in the courtroom. In R. P. Roberts, S. E. Carr and A. Dufour, eds., *The Critical Link 2: Interpreters in the Community: Selected Papers from the Second International Conference on Interpreting in Legal, Health, and Social Service Settings*. Amsterdam: John Benjamins, pp. 131–48.

Kenesei, A. (2010). *Poetry Translation through Reception and Cognition: The Proof of Translation is in the Reading*, Newcastle: Cambridge Scholars.

Koskinen, K. & Paloposki, O. (2015). Anxieties of influence: The voice of the first translator in retranslation. *Target*, 27(1), 25–39.

Kotze, H., Janssen, B., Koolen, C., van der Plas, L. & van Egdom, G.-W. (2021). Norms, affect and evaluation in the reception of literary translations in multilingual online reading communities: Deriving cognitive-evaluative templates from big data. *Translation, Cognition & Behavior*, 4(2), 147–86.

Kovačič, I. (1995). Reception of subtitles: The non-existent ideal viewer. *Translatio*, 14(3–4), 376–83.

Krejtz, I., Szarkowska, A. & Krejtz, K. (2013). The effects of shot changes on eye movements in subtitling. *Journal of Eye Movement Research*, 6(5), 1–12.

Kruger, H. (2012). *Postcolonial Polysystems: The Production and Reception of Translated Theoretical Advances*: Children's Literature in South Africa, Amsterdam: John Benjamins.

Kruger, H. (2013). Child and adult readers' processing of foreignised elements in translated South African picturebooks: An eye-tracking study. *Target*, 25(2), 180–227.

Kruger, H. (2016). Fluency/resistancy and domestication/foreignisation: A cognitive perspective. *Target*, 28(1), 4–41.

Kruger, H. & Kruger, J.-L. (2017). Cognition and reception. In J. Schwieter and A. Ferreira, eds., *The Handbook of Translation and Cognition*. Hoboken, NJ: John Wiley and Sons, pp. 71–89.

Kruger, J.-L. (2009). The translation of narrative fiction: Impostulating the narrative origo. *Perspectives*, 17(1), 155–32.

Kruger, J.-L. & Doherty, S. (2018). Triangulation of online and offline measures of processing and reception in AVT. In E. Di Giovanni and Y. Gambier, eds., *Reception Studies and Audiovisual Translation*. Amsterdam: John Benjamins, pp. 91–109.

Kruger, J.-L., Doherty, S. & Ibrahim, R. (2017). Electroencephalographic beta coherence as an objective measure of psychological immersion in film. *Rivista Internazionale di Tecnica della Traduzione/International Journal of Translation*, 19, 99–111.

Kruger, J.-L. & Liao, S. (2022). Establishing a theoretical framework for AVT research. The importance of cognitive models. *Translation Spaces*, 11(1), 12–37.

Kruger, J.-L., Wisniewska, N. & Liao, S. (2022). Why subtitle speed matters: Evidence from word skipping and rereading. *Applied Psycholinguistics*, 43(1), 211–36.

Kurz, I. (1993). Conference interpretation: Expectations of different user groups. *The Interpreters' Newsletter*, 5, 13–21.

Kurz, I. & Pöchhacker, F. (1995). Quality in TV interpreting. *Translatio*, 14(3/4), 350–8.

Lenglet, C. & Michaux, C. (2020). The impact of simultaneous-interpreting prosody on comprehension. An experiment. *Interpreting*, 22(1), 1–34.

Leppihalme, R. (1997). *Culture Bumps: An Empirical Approach to the Translation of Allusions*. London: Multilingual Matters.

Lewis, P. E. (1985/2012). The measure of translation effects. In L. Venuti, ed., *The Translation Studies Reader*, 3rd ed. London: Routledge, pp. 220–39.

Li, J. (2024). Reception of audiovisual translation in China: A survey study. *Perspectives*, 1–21. https://doi.org/10.1080/0907676X.2024.2361269.

Li, W. (2018). The image of H. C. Andersen's Tales in China (1909–1925): A case study of a set of key cultural texts in translation. In K. Malmkjær, A. Șerban and F. Louwagie, eds., *Key Cultural Texts in Translation*. Amsterdam: John Benjamins, pp. 153–70.

Lianeri, A. (2006). The Homeric moment? Translation, historicity, and the meaning of the classics. In C. Martindale and R. F. Thomas, eds., *Classics and the Uses of Reception*. Oxford: Blackwell, pp. 141–52.

Liang, W. (2007). A descriptive study of translating children's fantasy fiction. *Perspectives: Studies in Translatology*, 15(2), 92–105.

Liao S., Yu L., Kruger J. –L. & Reichle E. D. (2022). The impact of audio on the reading of intralingual versus interlingual subtitles: Evidence from eye movements. *Applied Psycholinguistics*, 43(1), 237–69.

Liao, S., Yu, L., Reichle, E. D. & Kruger, J.-L. (2021). Using eye movements to study the reading of subtitles in video. *Scientific Studies of Reading*, 25(5), 417–35.

Lindlof, T. R., Coyle, K. & Grodin, D. (1998). Is there a text in this audience? Science fiction and interpretive schism. In C. Harris and A. Alexander, eds., *Theorizing Fandom: Fans, Subculture and Identity*. New York: Hampton Press, pp. 219–48.

Lippi-Green, R. (1997). *English with an Accent: Language, Ideology, and Discrimination in the United States*, London: Psychology Press.

Liu, B. & Baer, B. J. (2017). Packaging a Chinese 'beauty writer': Re-reading Shanghai Baby in a web context. *Meta*, 62(2), 415–34.

Liu, M. (2023). User expectations research revisited: Methodological considerations. In C. Zwischenberger, K. Reithofer and S. Rennert, eds., *Introducing New Hypertexts on Interpreting (Studies): A tribute to Franz Pöchhacker*. Amsterdam: John Benjamins, pp. 44–65.

Mack, G. & Cattaruzza, L. (1995). User surveys in SI: A means of learning about quality and/or raising some reasonable doubts. In J. Tommola, ed., *Topics in Interpreting Research*. Turku: University of Turku, Centre for Translation and Interpreting, pp. 37–49.

Marais, K. (2019). *A (Bio)Semiotic Theory of Translation: The Emergence of Social-Cultural Reality*, New York: Routledge.

Martindale, C. (2006). Introduction: Thinking through reception. In C. Martindale and R. F. Thomas, eds., *Classics and the Uses of Reception*. Oxford: Blackwell, pp. 1–13.

Mason, I. (2000). Audience design in translating. *The Translator*, 6(1), 1–22.

Matamala, A. & Ortiz-Boix, C. (2016). Accessibility and multilingualism: An exploratory study on the machine translation of audio descriptions. *Revista de Traductología*, 20(20), 11–24.

Mazur, I. & Vercauteren, G. (2019). Media accessibility training. *Linguistica Antverpiensia, New Series – Themes in Translation Studies*, 18, 1–22.

Meylaerts, R. (2008). Translators and (their) norms: Towards a sociological construction of the individual. In M. Shlesinger, D. Simeoni and A. Pym, eds., *Beyond Description Translation Studies: Investigations in Homage to Gideon Toury*. Amsterdam: John Benjamins, pp. 91–102.

Mężyk, J. (2022). Simultaneous interpreting in Evangelical churches in Poland as an example of a non-professional practice. In M. Kornacki and G. Massey, eds., *Contextuality in Translation and Interpreting: Selected Papers from the Łódź-ZHAW Duo Colloquium on Translation and Meaning 2020–2021*. Berlin: Peter Lang, pp. 291–310.

Michelakis, P. (2006). Reception, performance, and the sacrifice of Iphigenia. In C. Martindale and R. F. Thomas, eds., *Classics and the Uses of Reception*. Oxford: Blackwell, pp. 124–226.

Mellinger, C. D. & T. A. Hanson. (2022). Considerations of ecological validity in cognitive translation and interpreting studies. *Translation, Cognition & Behavior*, 5(1), 1–26.

Milton, J. & Bandia, P. F. (2009). *Agents of translation*, Amsterdam: John Benjamins.

Monzó-Nebot, E. & Mellinger, C. D. (2022). Language policies for social justice – Translation, interpreting, and access. *Just. Journal of Language Rights & Minorities, Revista De Drets Lingüístics I Minories*, 1(1–2), 15–35.

Moran, S. (2012). The effect of linguistic variation on subtitle reception. In E. Perego, ed., *Eye Tracking in Audiovisual Translation*. Rome: Aracne, pp. 183–222.

Moser, P. (1996). Expectations of users of conference interpretation. *Interpreting*, 1(2), 145–78.

Muñoz Martín, R. (2010). On paradigms and cognitive translatology. In G. Shreve and E. Angelone, eds., *Translation and Cognition*. Amsterdam: John Benjamins, pp. 169–87.

Naughton, J. (2004). *Always Time for a Change*, www.theguardian.com/technology/2004/jan/04/business.theobserver.

Neveu, A. (2017). How paratexts influence the reader's experience of English translations of La Fontaine's Fables. *New Voices in Translation Studies*, 16, 23–54.

Newmark, P. (1988). Pragmatic Translation and Literalism. *TTR: Traduction, Terminologie, Rédaction*, 1, 133–45. https://doi.org/10.7202/037027ar.

Newmark, P. (1997). The customer as king. *Current Issues in Language and Society*, 4(1), 75–7.

Nida, E. A. & Taber, C. R. (2003/1969). *The Theory and Practice of Translation*, Leiden: Brill.

Nord, C. (2001). Loyalty revisited: Bible translation as a case in point. *The Translator*, 7(2), 185–202.

Nord, C. (2005). *Text Analysis in Translation: Theory, Methodology and Didactic Application of a Model for Translation-Oriented Text Analysis*, Amsterdam: Rodopi.

O'Sullivan, E. (2012). Children's literature and translation studies. In C. Millán and F. Bartrina, eds., *The Routledge Handbook of Translation Studies*. New York: Routledge, pp. 469–81.

Padilla, P., Bajo, M. T. & Padilla, F. (1999). Proposal for a cognitive theory of translation and interpreting: A methodology for future empirical research. *The Interpreters' Newsletter*, 9, 61–78.

Pavesi, M. (2019). Dubbing. In M. Baker and G. Saldanha, eds., *Routledge Encyclopedia of Translation Studies*, 3rd ed. London: Routledge, pp. 156–61.

Pedersen, J. (2017). The FAR model: Assessing quality in interlingual subtitling. *Journal of Specialised Translation*, 28, 210–29.

Perego, E., Del Missier, F., Porta, M. & Mosconi, M. (2010). The cognitive effectiveness of subtitle processing. *Media Psychology*, 13(3), 243–72.

Pérez-Luzardo Díaz, J. (2015). The style parameter in quality evaluation and expectations of simultaneous interpreting. *Sendebar*, 26, 213–33.

Pillemer, D. B. (2001). Momentous events and the life story. *Review of General Psychology*, 5(2), 123–34.

Pöchhacker, F. (2002). Researching interpreting quality: Models and methods. In G. Garzone and M. Viezzi, eds., *Interpreting in the 21st Century: Challenges and Opportunities*. Amsterdam: Routledge, pp. 95–106.

Pöchhacker, F. (2005). Quality research revisited. *The Interpreters' Newsletter*, 13, 143–66.

Pöchhacker, F. (2015). User expectations. In F. Pöchhacker, ed., *Routledge Encyclopedia of Interpreting Studies*. London: Routledge, pp. 430–2.

Pöchhacker, F. (2018). Media interpreting. From user expectations to audience comprehension. In E. Di Giovanni and Y. Gambier, eds., *Reception Studies and Audiovisual Translation*. Amsterdam: John Benjamins, pp. 253–76.

Putnam, R. D. (2000). *Bowling Alone – the Collapse and Revival of American Community*, 1st ed., New York: Simon & Schuster Paperbacks.

Puurtinen, T. (1994). Dynamic style as a parameter of acceptability in translated children's books. In M. Snell-Hornby, F. Pöchhacker and K. Kaindl, eds., *Translation Studies: An Interdiscipline*. Amsterdam: John Benjamins, pp. 83–90.

Pym, A. (2015). Translating as risk management. *Journal of Pragmatics*, 85, 67–80.

Pym, A. (2020). Translation, risk management and cognition. In F. Alves and A. Lykke Jakobsen, eds., *The Routledge Handbook of Translation and Cognition*. London: Routledge, pp. 445–58.

Pym, A. (2025). *Risk Management in Translation*, Cambridge: Cambridge University Press.

Pym, A., Ayvazyan, N. & Prioleau, J. (2022). Should raw machine translation be used for public-health information? Suggestions for a multilingual communication policy in Catalonia. *Just. Journal of Language Rights & Minorities, Revista de Drets Lingüístics i Minories*, 1(1–2), 71–99.

Pym, A. & Hu, B. (2022). Trust and cooperation through social media. COVID-19 translations for Chinese communities in Melbourne. In T. K. Lee and D. Wang, eds., *Translation and Social Media Communication in the Age of the Pandemic*. Abingdon: Routledge, pp. 44–61.

Pym, A. & Hu, K. (2025). Trade-offs in translation effects. Illustrations and methodological concerns. Target, 1(37), 117–28.

Qiu, J. & Pym, A. (2024). Fatal flaws? Investigating the effects of machine translation errors on audience reception in the audiovisual context. *Perspectives*, 1–17. https://doi.org/10.1080/0907676X.2024.2328757.

Rajendran, D. J., Duchowski, A. T., Orero, P., Martínez, J. & Romero-Fresco, P. (2013). Effects of Text Chunking on Subtitling: A Quantitative and Qualitative Examination. *Perspectives*, 21(1), 5–21.

Rebora, S., Boot, P., Pianzola, F., et al. (2021). Digital humanities and digital social reading. *Digital Scholarship in the Humanities*, 36(Supplement_2), 230–50.

Reichle, E. D. (2021). *Computational Models of Reading: A Handbook*, Oxford: Oxford University Press.

Reiss, K. & Vermeer, H. (1984). *Groundwork for a General Theory of Translation*, Tubingen: Niemeyer.

René de Cotret, F., Brisset, C. & Leanza, Y. (2021). A typology of healthcare interpreter positionings: When 'neutral' means 'proactive'. *Interpreting*, 23(1), 103–26.

Rimmon-Kenan, S. (2002). *Narrative Fiction, Contemporary Poetics*, 2nd ed., London: Routledge.

Rizzi, A., Lang, B. & Pym, A. (2019). *What Is Translation History? A Trust-Based Approach*, Cham: Palgrave Macmillan.

Robbins, P. & Aydede, M. (2009). A short primer on situated cognition. In P. Robbins and M. Aydede, eds., *The Cambridge Handbook of Situated Cognition*. Cambridge: Cambridge University Press, pp. 3–10.

Robinson, D. (2020). Reframing translational norm theory through 4EA cognition. *Translation, Cognition & Behavior*, 3(1), 122–42.

Rojo, A., Ramos, M. & Valenzuela, J. (2014). The emotional impact of translation: A heart rate study. *Journal of Pragmatics*, 71, 31–44.

Romero-Fresco, P. (ed.) (2015). *The Reception of Subtitles for the Deaf and Hard of Hearing in Europe*, New York: Peter Lang.

Romero-Fresco, P. & Pöchhacker. F. (2017). Quality assessment in interlingual live subtitling: The NTR model. *Linguistica Antverpiensia, New Series: Themes in Translation Studies*, 16, 149–67.

Romero-Fresco, P. & Dangerfield, K. (2022). Accessibility as a conversation. *Journal of Audiovisual Translation*, 5(2), 15–34.

Rowberry, S. P. (2016). Commonplacing the public domain: Reading the classics socially on the Kindle. *Language and Literature*, 25(3), 211–25.

Russo, M. (2005). Simultaneous film interpreting and users' feedback. *Interpreting*, 7(1), 1–26.

Santesso, A. (2006). *A Careful Longing: The Poetics and Problems of Nostalgia*, Newark, NJ: University of Delaware Press.

Sela-Sheffy, R. (2005). How to be a (recognized) translator: Rethinking habitus, norms, and the field of translation. *Target*, 17(1), 1–26.

Setton, R. & Dawrant, A. (2016). *Conference Interpreting: A Trainer's Guide*, Amsterdam: John Benjamins.

Seymour, R. (2019). *The Twittering Machine: How Capitalism Stole Our Social Life*, London: Indigo Press.

Slomczynski, K. M., Tomescu-Dubrow, I., Jenkins, J. C. & Wolf, C. (2024). Objectives and challenges of survey data harmonization. In I. Tomescu-Dubrow, C. Wolf, K. M. Slomczynski and J. C. Jenkins, eds., *Survey Data Harmonization in the Social Sciences*. New York: Wiley, pp. 1–20.

Snell-Hornby, M. (2005). Of catfish and blue bananas: Scenes-and-frames semantics as a contrastive 'knowledge system' for translation. In H. V. Dam,

J. Engberg and H. Gerzymisch-Arbogast, eds., *Knowledge Systems and Translation*. Berlin: Mouton de Gruyter, pp. 193–206.

Staiger, J. (2005). *Media Reception Studies*, New York, NY: New York University Press.

Sternberg, R. J. & Sternberg, K. (2016). *Cognitive Psychology*, Boston, MA: Cengage Learning.

Stevens, S. S. (1946). On the theory of scales of measurement. *Science*, 103(2684), 677–80.

Suojanen, T., Koskinen, K. & Tuominen, T. (2015). *User-Centered Translation*, London: Routledge.

Szarkowska, A. & Boczkowska, J. (2022). Colour coding subtitles in multilingual films – A reception study. *Perspectives*, 30(3), 520–36.

Szarkowska, A. & Gerber-Morón, O. (2018). Viewers can keep up with fast subtitles: Evidence from eye movements. *PLoS ONE*, 13(6), e0199331.

Szarkowska, A., Krejtz, I., Kłyszejko, Z. & Wieczorek, A. (2011). Verbatim, standard, or edited? Reading patterns of different captioning styles among deaf, hard of hearing, and hearing viewers. *American Annals of the Deaf*, 156(4), 363–78.

Szarkowska, A., Ragni, V., Szkriba, S., Black, S., Kruger, J.-L. & Orrego-Carmona, D. (2024). 'That's not what they said!' The impact of incongruities between the dialogue and intralingual subtitles on viewer experience. *Perspectives*, 1–20. https://doi.org/10.1080/0907676X.2024.2386040.

Szarkowska, A., Ragni, V., Szkriba, S., Black, S., Orrego-Carmona, D. & Kruger, J.-L. (2024). Watching subtitled videos with the sound off affects viewers' comprehension, cognitive load, immersion, enjoyment, and gaze patterns: A mixed-methods eye-tracking study. *PLoS ONE*, 19(10), e0306251.

Tamborini, R., Bowman, N. D., Eden, A., Grizzard, M. & Organ, A. (2010). Defining media enjoyment as the satisfaction of intrinsic needs. *Journal of Communication*, 60, 758–77.

Teas, R. K. (1993). Expectations, performance evaluation, and consumers' perceptions of quality. *Journal of Marketing*, 57(4), 18–34.

Tekgül, D. (2019). Book club meetings as micro public spheres: Translated literature and cosmopolitanism. *Language and Intercultural Communication*, 19(5), 380–92.

Thelwall, M. (2019). Reader and author gender and genre in Goodreads. *Journal of Librarianship and Information Science*, 51(2), 403–30.

Toury, G. (1980). *In Search of a Theory of Translation*. Tel Aviv: Porter Institute for Poetics and Semiotics.

Toury, G. (1995/2012). *Descriptive Translation Studies and beyond*, 2nd ed., Amsterdam: John Benjamins.

Tuominen, T. (2018). Multi-method research: Reception in context. In E. Di Giovanni and Y. Gambier, eds., *Reception Studies and Audiovisual Translation*. Amsterdam: John Benjamins, pp. 69–90.

Tuominen, T., Koponen, M., Vitikainen, K., Sulubacak, U. & Tiedemann, J. (2023). Exploring the gaps in linguistic accessibility of media: The potential of automated subtitling as a solution. *Journal of Specialised Translation*, 39, 77–98.

Tymoczko, M. (2012). The neuroscience of translation. *Target*, 24(1), 83–102.

Valdez, S. (2023). On the reception of biomedical translation: Comparing and contrasting health professionals' evaluation of translation options and expectations about the safe use of medical devices in Portuguese. *The Translator*, 28(4), 538–54.

Valdez, S. Robles, L. P. & van den Berg, K. (2025). The reception of translated vaccination Information: Evidence from a reading and stops-making-sense judgment task. *Target*, 37(2), 213–43.

Valero-Garcés, C. (2022). Communicating in multilingual churches: The interpreter's role as a case study. *FORUM*, 20(2), 290–308.

Van Doorslaer, L. (2024). Translation (studies) and imagology. In S. Tyulenev and W. Luo, eds., *The Routledge Handbook of Translation and Sociology*. London: Routledge, pp. 447–59.

Venuti, L. (2008). *The Translator's Invisibility: A History of Translation*, 2nd ed., London: Routledge.

Vieira, L. N., O'Sullivan, C., Zhang, X. & O'Hagan, M. (2023). Machine translation in society: Insights from UK users. *Language Resources & Evaluation*, 57, 893–914.

Vilar, D., Xu, J., D'Haro, L. F. & Ney, H. (2006). 'Error analysis of statistical machine translation output'. In Proceedings of the Fifth International Conference on Language Resources and Evaluation (LREC'06), Genoa, Italy. European Language Resources Association (ELRA).

Walker, C. (2021). Investigating how we read. Translations: A call to action for experimental studies of translation reception. *Cognitive Linguistic Studies*, 8(2), 482–512.

Walker, C. & Federici, F. M. (2018). *Eye Tracking and Multidisciplinary Studies on Translation*, Amsterdam: John Benjamins.

Walsh, M. & Antoniak, M. (2021). The Goodreads 'classics': A computational study of readers, Amazon, and crowdsourced amateur criticism. *Journal of Cultural Analytics*, 4, 243–87.

Wang, F. & Humblé, P. (2020). Readers' perceptions of Anthony Yu's self-retranslation of The Journey to the West. *Perspectives*, 28(5), 756–76.

Wardle, M. L. (2012). Alice in busi-land: The reciprocal relation between text and paratext. In A. Gil-Bardaji, P. Orero and S. Rovira-Esteva, eds., *Translation Peripheries: Paratextual Elements in Translation*. Bern: Peter Lang, pp. 27–41.

Wardle, M. L. (2019). Uni Duni Tê: The reception of retranslations and how readers choose. *Cadernos de tradução*, 39(1), 216–38.

Wehrmeyer, J. (2014). Introducing grounded theory into translation studies. *Southern African Linguistics and Applied Language Studies*, 32(3), 373–87.

White, E. B. (1952). *Charlotte's Web*, New York: Harper & Brothers.

Whitehead, A. N. (1967). *Adventures of Ideas*, New York: Free Press.

Whyatt, B., Tomczak-Łukaszewska, E., Witczak, O. & Lehka-Paul, O. (2024). Readers have to work harder to understand a badly translated text: An eye-tracking study into the effects of translation errors. *Perspectives*, 1–21. https://doi.org/10.1080/0907676X.2024.2418016.

Xiao, X., Chen, X. & Palmer, J. L. (2015). Chinese deaf viewers' comprehension of sign language interpreting on television: An experimental study. *Interpreting*, 17(1), 91–117.

Yang, Y. (2020). The Danmaku interface on Bilibili and the recontextualised translation practice: A semiotic technology perspective. *Social Semiotics*, 30(2), 254–73.

Yang, Y. (2023). *Danmu* as archi-text and meta-text: A semiotic analysis of online video consumption shaped by viewers' (translational) comments. *Translation Studies*, 16(3), 398–418.

Zárate, S. (2021). *Captioning and Subtitling for d/Deaf and Hard of Hearing Audiences*. London: UCL Press.

Zasyekin, S. (2010). Translation as psycholinguistic phenomenon. *Journal of Psycholinguistic Research*, 39, 225–34.

Zwischenberger, C. (2013). *Qualität und Rollenbilder beim simultanen Konferenzdolmetschen* [Quality and role models in simultaneous conference interpreting], Berlin: Frank und Timme.

Acknowledgement

This Element, which focuses on the reception of translation, has been years in the making. It has been a journey of curiosity, experimentation, and writing, and I have accumulated an innumerable debt of gratitude.

My fascination with how *people* respond to translated texts, whether in the configurations of political discourse, health communication, or interpreting, was kindled during my doctoral studies in Melbourne. As I drafted some early papers on risk analysis of high-stakes translation reception, I found myself drawn to an intriguing question: How does trust condition the very way a translation is accepted? The quest for a more integrated, socio-cognitive approach to translation reception has since guided me on the path that culminates in this Element.

The journey, as is often the case with intellectual pursuits, has been anything but linear. Along the way, I have been fortunate to engage in countless dialogues with colleagues in Melbourne, Singapore, Paris, Vienna, Hong Kong, and beyond. Some offered critical critique, others words of encouragement, but all contributed to the formation of the ideas presented here. Among these remarkable individuals, two stand out for their tremendous support and long-term engagement with my academic career: Anthony Pym and Andrew Chesterman. Their generosity, both in time and in intellect, has been a constant source of inspiration. They offered thoughtful feedback, reading drafts with great care and offering prescient advice with boundless kindness.

Anthony, as my PhD supervisor, has been a guiding light throughout. He spent countless hours discussing the reception project with me in Melbourne and, afterwards, years of reflection on the concept of trust in translation as he answered my seemingly endless questions. Andrew is the one who, without fail, would insist, 'Bei! I'm retired!' every time I emailed him a copy of a new book on translation. Nevertheless, within twenty minutes, I'd find myself receiving a thoughtful, and always critical, review of the book – proof that retirement, for Andrew, was merely a suggestion. Their insights have shaped the very way I think about the relationship between translator, text, and reader, particularly in a world where ideologies diverge and yet common ground remains, waiting to be discovered, tested, and shared.

The Department of Chinese Studies at the National University of Singapore graciously provided the opportunity for a writing leave, without which this work would not have come to fruition. Macquarie University offered the cognitive laboratory and office space that allowed me the time and quiet to write, learn new cognitive approaches to reception from local colleagues, and fine-tune my ideas.

I also wish to extend my sincere thanks to the editors at Cambridge Elements and to the anonymous reviewers. Their editorial care and sharp insights have refined this manuscript in ways I could never have achieved alone.

This work was supported by the Singapore Ministry of Education (MOE) Tier 1 Grant (Grant No. FY2023-FRC2-002) and the FASS Book Grant Scheme (FY2024) at the National University of Singapore.

To all of you, I am profoundly grateful.

Cambridge Elements ≡

Translation and Interpreting

The series is edited by Kirsten Malmkjær with Sabine Braun as associate editor for Elements focusing on Interpreting.

Kirsten Malmkjær
University of Leicester

Kirsten Malmkjær is Professor Emeritus of Translation Studies at the University of Leicester. She has taught Translation Studies at the universities of Birmingham, Cambridge, Middlesex and Leicester and has written extensively on aspects of both the theory and practice of the discipline. *Translation and Creativity* (London: Routledge) was published in 2020 and *The Cambridge Handbook of Translation*, which she edited, was published in 2022. She is preparing a volume entitled *Introducing Translation* for the Cambridge Introductions to Language and Linguistics series.

Editorial Board

Adriana Serban, *Université Paul Valéry*
Barbara Ahrens, *Technische Hochschule Köln*
Liu Min-Hua, *Hong Kong Baptist University*
Christine Ji, *The University of Sydney*
Jieun Lee, *Ewha Womans University*
Lorraine Leeson, *The University of Dublin*
Sara Laviosa, *Università Delgi Stuidi di Bari Aldo Moro*
Fabio Alves, *FALE-UFMG*
Moira Inghilleri, *University of Massachusetts Amherst*
Akiko Sakamoto, *University of Portsmouth*
Haidee Kotze, *Utrecht University*

About the Series

Elements in Translation and Interpreting present cutting edge studies on the theory, practice and pedagogy of translation and interpreting. The series also features work on machine learning and AI, and human-machine interaction, exploring how they relate to multilingual societies with varying communication and accessibility needs, as well as text-focused research.

Cambridge Elements

Translation and Interpreting

Elements in the Series

Interpreting as Translanguaging
Lili Han, Zhisheng (Edward) Wen and Alan James Runcieman

Creative Classical Translation
Paschalis Nikolaou

Translation as Creative–Critical Practice
Delphine Grass

Translation in Analytic Philosophy
Francesca Ervas

Towards Game Translation User Research
Mikołaj Deckert, Krzysztof Wiesław Hejduk, and Miguel Ángel Bernal-Merino

An Extraordinary Chinese Translation of Holocaust Testimony
Meiyuan Zhao

Hypertranslation
África Vidal Claramonte and Tong King Lee

Researching and Modelling the Translation Process
Muhammad M. M. Abdel Latif

Risk Management in Translation
Anthony Pym

Literary Exophonic Translation
Lúcia Collischonn

Charting Translation Reception: Methods and Challenges
Bei Hu

A full series listing is available at: www.cambridge.org/EITI

Printed by Integrated Books International,
United States of America